CISTERCIAN STUDIES SERIES : NUMBER TWO

THE
MONASTIC THEOLOGY
OF
AELRED OF RIEVAULX

CISTERCIAN STUDIES SERIES

CISTERCIAN STUDIES SERIES : NUMBER TWO

Amédée Hallier ocso

THE
MONASTIC THEOLOGY
OF
AELRED OF RIEVAULX

An Experiential Theology

translated by Columban Heaney ocso

with a special introduction by Thomas Merton

translations from Aelred's works by
Hugh McCaffery ocso

SHANNON · IRELAND
1969

This book was first published by
J. Gabalda & Cie.
under the title
Un Éducateur Monastique, Aelred de Rievaulx.

Ecclesiastical permission to publish this translation was received from
M. Ignace Gillet, Abbot General of the Cistercian Order, and Bernard
Flanagan, Bishop of Worcester, January 6, 1969.

SBN 7165 0599 1

Irish University Press Shannon Ireland
DUBLIN CORK BELFAST LONDON NEW YORK
Captain T M MacGlinchey publisher
Robert Hogg printer

Printed in the Republic of Ireland by
Cahill & Co. Limited, Parkgate Printing Works, Dublin

CONTENTS

ABBREVIATIONS

Am.	*De Spirituali Amicitia*, ed. J. Dubois (Paris: Beyaert, 1948); *On Spiritual Friendship*, trans. Sr Rose of Lima, *The Works of Aelred of Rievaulx*, vol. 2 (Cistercian Fathers Series, 5).
Anima	*Tractatus de Anima*, ed. C. H. Talbot (London: Warburg Institute, 1952).
Inst.	*De Institutis Inclusarum*, ed. C. H. Talbot in *Analecta Sacri Ordinis Cisterciensis*, VII (1951) pp. 167–217; *The Life of the Recluse*, in *The Works of Aelred of Rievaulx*, vol. 1 (Cistercian Fathers Series, 2).
Jesu	*Tractatus de Jesu puero duodenni*, ed. A. Hoste (Paris: Cerf, 1958), *Sources Chrétiennes*, No. 60; *When Jesus Was Twleve*, in *The Works of Aelred of Rieaulx*, vol. 1 (Cistercian Fathers Series, 2).
O. Past.	*Oratio Pastoralis*, ed. C. Dumont (Paris: Cerf, 1961), *Sources chrétiennes*, No. 76; *The Pastoral Prayer of Saint Aelred of Rievaulx*, trans. Religious of CSMV (Westminster: Dacre, 1955).
S. Ined.	*Sermones Inediti*, ed. C. H. Talbot (Rome: S.O. Cisterciensis, 1952).
S. Oner.	*Sermones de Oneribus*, P. L. 195, 361–500.
S. Temp.	*Sermones de Tempore et de Sanctis*, P. L. 195, 210–360.
Spec.	*Speculum Caritatis*, P. L. 195, 504–620; *Mirror of Charity*, trans. G. Webb and A. Walker (London: Mowbray, 1962), *incomplete*.
Vita	Walter Daniel's Life of Ailred (*Vita Ailredi*), ed. and trans. F. M. Powicke (London: Nelson, 1950).

Note: In the series of sermons *De Oneribus*, the numbering adopted differs by one from that given by Migne. Sermon 1 in Migne is really the sermon *The Lord's Coming (De Adventu Domini)*.

INTRODUCTION

by

Thomas Merton

The postconciliar era is favorable for the rediscovery of monastic theology. Not only have monks been urged to return to their sources and rethink their vocation in terms both of the original charism and of present needs, but also pre-scholastic theology can now be seen in much better perspective. As long as scholasticism occupied the entire Catholic theological landscape, blocking out everything else, with the Bible and the Fathers seen only in relation to its all-embracing system, there was small chance of the monastic theologians getting due attention. They were regarded as obscure and irrelevant scribes who had nothing original to add to the predecessors they merely copied. St Bernard was of course respected in the domain of "spirituality" (whatever that was) and St Anselm was mentioned in textbooks as an abbot with a flair for dialectic who had made a pass at scholastic thinking and missed. But by and large the theology of the west between St Augustine and Peter Lombard was regarded as a wasteland.

It was not until the nineteen forties and fifties—largely with the work of Dom Jean Leclercq—that the real value of the post-patristic writers in the monasteries of the west began to be rediscovered. Where we had assumed there were only trite catalogs of allegory we found again a literature rich in biblical culture, a genuine theology and a humanism full of psychological insight with plenty of relevance for our own day.

However, this does not mean that "monastic theology" has yet come into its own in America. The Middle Ages are still regarded with understandable misgivings because in America the word "medieval" refers in fact to the pseudo-medieval mishmash of romanticism, conservatism and authoritarianism whose epiphany was the pseudo-Gothic parish church in an ethnic ghetto, giving itself the airs of a cathedral though dwarfed by the surrounding factories.

Even in monasteries, where people might be expected to know better, the monastic theologians of the twelfth century have been honored rather than studied and have thus become part of the discredited medieval myth.

Studies like the present one of Fr Amédée Hallier now make it possible for us to get an entirely new view of medieval monasticism and we can understand why M.-D. Chenu, still one of the best modern theologians, insists that a knowledge of pre-scholastic theology is necessary to balance "a certain spiritual and apostolic pragmatism" in current thinking.

Let us be quite clear that the monastic theology of Aelred is not a partisan "theology of monasticism." It is not an apologia for the life of the monk, not a kind of gnostic system organized to prove some supposed superiority of "the contemplative life," urging a flight to ineffable convulsions.

A "monastic theology" is the fruit not of a special kind of speculation but of a deeply lived experience of the mysteries of faith. The aim of medieval monasticism was not simply to gain heaven by rejection of the world (for after all history shows how deeply involved the monks were in the world of their time) but a positive witness to the presence of Christ in the world. The monastic witness was not so much ascetic as eschatological. Not so much a denial of man and the flesh as an affirmation of the Word made Flesh, taking all created things to himself, in order to transform and fulfill them in himself. Hence the monastic theology of the Cistercian and Benedictine writers of the eleventh and twelfth centuries is highly concrete, existential, biblical, imaginatively rich, full of esthetic as well as mystical intuitions, and deeply rooted in the everyday life of the time. It is concerned above all not with abstract ideas about God but with the living relationship of man with God in Christ. And this of course meant an overriding concern with the love of man for man—that love by which we are known as Christ's disciples, without which there is no "life in Christ" and therefore no union with God.

Aelred's pedagogy centers on the formation of the whole man, not as an individual but as a member of a community. Monastic theology is before all else a theology of community. It implies a certain definite concept of man which it would be well to sketch out here.

Man is in his basic structure *capax Dei*. He is an openness, a capacity, a possibility, a freedom, whose fulfillment is not in this or that isolated object, this or that circumscribed activity, but in a fullness beyond all "objects," the totality of consent and self-giving which is love. God is Love. Man is an openness that is fulfilled only in unconditional consent to an unconditional love. This openness, this freedom, which is at the very core of man's being—and which imperiously demands that he transcend his being—is what the monastic theologians call the image of God in man. The capacity for freedom and love is the image of God because God himself is pure freedom and pure love. The image in man—the openness that demands to transcend itself in love—seeks to attain a perfect likeness to its original by loving as it is loved. It cannot of course attain this by its own nature. But God has given his own Son that we may be sons in him. The coming of the Word to take our freedom to himself turns the "image" into "likeness." When the Word loves the Father in us, then our freedom is transfigured in and by his Spirit, and our love becomes identical with his love. This implies perfection of pure consent, and the monastery is a school where men devote their lives to learning and practicing this consent. *Consentire salvari est,* said St Bernard in his tract on Free Will and Grace, and his whole theology of love is a theology of *consensus*, like-minded-ness, unity of hearts and wills, first on the communal level and then in that mystical community of persons where the Christian (individually and ecclesially) is caught up into participation with the triune inner life of God himself. Perfect consent in the visible and everyday life of the monastic community—a life of work in close contact with matter and nature, a life of prayer and praise rich in biblical symbol and human art—makes possible an epiphany of the invisible redemptive presence of God, in whom Three Persons are One inexhaustible consent. The visible Christian community (to realize which is the life work of the cenobite) is the fulfillment of Christ's highpriestly prayer: "May they all be one in us, Father, as you are in me and I am in you, so that the world may believe that it was you that sent me" (John 17:21).

The image of God in man—the openness to love, the capacity for total consent to God in himself and in others—remains indestructible. But it can be buried and imprisoned under selfishness. The image of God in man is not destroyed by sin but utterly disfigured by it. To be exact, the image of God in man becomes self-contradictory when its openness closes in upon itself, when it ceases to be a capacity for love and becomes simply an appetite for domination or possession: when it ceases to give and seeks only to get. In such a case, man becomes his own god and instead of loving others he uses them for his own purposes—to gratify his own narcissism as we would say today. The early Cistercians had some very refined insights into the regressive, sado-masochistic evasions by which men disguise and justify their infidelity to the inmost truth in themselves. The real root of sin, as they saw with Augustine, is close to Sartre's "bad faith" in its actual structure: it is a lying misuse of one's own freedom, turning it against itself and sabotaging it while pretending to affirm it. In monastic terms: the inclination to love, which is at the core of man's very nature as a free being, is turned in on itself as its own object and ceases to be love. When an individual freedom seeks to be its own sufficient reason for existence it ceases to be free (and here we might explore the ambiguities of freedom in the context of a loveless existentialism!).

The purpose of monastic education is, in plain terms, the education of authentic freedom by loving and creative consent. Since man is made for love, his love has to be liberated, guided, educated, directed not to objects which end in blind alleys but to *other loves* which in their free and creative response call forth more love in ourselves. In other words, love is educated by other loves, freedom by consent to, consensus with, other freedoms. At first this implies a certain difficulty and constraint. There is need of monastic discipline because the spontaneous freedom of love has been lost: egotism and narcissism have corrupted our "taste" for freedom. What we "experience" as freedom and as love is too often selfishness and self-involvement, masking as love for others. Not only must consciences be formed but one must learn to experience, to "taste" the difference between freedom and unfreedom, love and selfishness. We might mention that this "discernment of spirits" is very important in the actual working out of problems in monastic renewal today. We all know that merely authoritarian and legalistic solutions are no longer adequate. But on the other hand we have been so long held up by authoritarian structures that many of us have no idea of how to function without them. Hence, though there is much talk of freedom and love, there is in fact a great deal of infantile and narcissistic authoritarianism at work precisely where everything claims to be most open-ended and most free. The only way to guard against this is by a really serious and patient discipline of love. Aelred writes about that discipline, which alone can restore that intimate "taste" for true freedom and authentic love, the *sapor boni* which is essential to wisdom and to "contemplation."

The thing that is most characteristic of Aelred's monastic theology is its emphasis on friendship. His doctrine is not simply a theology of community but a *theology of friendship*. The Christian life is, for Aelred, simply the full flowering of freedom and consent in the perfection of friendship. Friendship with other human beings as an epiphany of friendship with God. In this, surely, he is quite modern. "To live without friends," he says, "is to live like a beast." For this very reason—we must dare to admit it—he was for a long time regarded as "dangerous" in certain monasteries. Not so long ago, some of Aelred's books were kept under lock and key in Trappist libraries—just as John of the Cross was kept locked up in some Carmels.

It is significant indeed when a writer who has gone to the very heart of the monastic vocation has to be kept out of the hands of monks lest they be "troubled" by his insights!

For Aelred, the monastic community life is simply a life of friendship. The monastic discipline is an education in friendship. Contemplation is not an individual gnostic exploit arrived at by turning away from everybody else to God: it is a sharing in the friendship of God. The love of the monk for his brothers is the ground of a common contemplative experience of Christ. Friendship is then not an obstacle to some supposed "spiritual perfection": friendship itself is Christian perfection. But it has to be true friendship, not a fake.

The natural basis for this theology of friendship is of course the indestructible inclination to love which is the divine image in us. But we have seen that this inclination tends to frustrate and to caricature itself by unconscious bad faith, selfishness, narcissism, inauthenticity and pretense. The seriousness of this danger cannot be overestimated and no amount of psychotherapy or sensitivity sessions can entirely overcome it. We must of course take advantage of all the psychological and sociological instruments at our disposal, but ultimately, as Aelred says, our love is healed and redirected only in Christ. Only in him is the divine image, our freedom, restored to likeness in authenticity and truth—*in veritate caritatis*. He alone gives the true gift of community. Friendship is not the flowering of our inborn needs: it is God's creation. An entirely new creation in Christ. Our wounded and broken love is inclined to hate even when it thinks it loves. This brokenness and ambivalence can be healed only in the Holy Spirit. Our healing comes from the Cross. It is the gift of the Risen Savior. All this Aelred makes plain. And we must not forget it in a day when the temptation to be satisfied with an entirely horizontal dimension in theology may only compound our troubles instead of getting rid of them.

We might close by quoting a modern evangelical theologian whose name is so often invoked in favor of this "horizontal" theology, concerned only with man's relation to man. People easily forget that Bonhoeffer was well aware of man's brokenness and of his need for grace. He said: "God and reality are torn apart except where they come together in Christ." The statement echoes Aelred's description of true friendship.

Aelred's monastic pedagogy is anything but a training in blindness and rejection. It is a training in openness and consent, a training in outgoing acceptance. But he demands acceptance first of all of Christ and his Cross. It is in Christ, and only in him, that the world makes sense. But once we have surrendered to Christ and to his saving Word, then Aelred would agree perfectly with Bonhoeffer: "Whoever sees Jesus Christ does indeed see God and the world in one. He can thenceforward no longer see God without the world or the world without God."

FOREWORD

This book on St Aelred by Fr Amédée Hallier is set in the context of a renewal that is in reality a rediscovery. In the Church today there is a growing interest in the origins and in the early witnesses of Christianity, as a result of which we are becoming more and more aware that the doctrinal tradition stemming from these sources was preserved, developed and enriched by the represent- atives of what can justly be called medieval patristic theology. Many of these were monks, in particular those who lived in the twelfth century and came under the magnetic influence of St Bernard, "the last of the Fathers." But before they wrote, indeed in order to be able to write, these men had lived and experienced what they taught. The work presented here puts us in touch with one such life in all its exuberant vitality.

If St Bernard is the greatest, the most brilliant and the most original of these spiritual masters, he is by that very fact far from being the easiest to approach. His richness at times dazzles us by its very brilliance, at other times is concealed beneath poetic forms that are so intricate as to be perplexing. St Aelred is closer to us, certainly closer to the mentality of the English-speaking world. Accordingly, quite apart from the interest which he offers in himself, he can do us the service of introducing us to Bernard and other theologians whose doctrine is more involved or more difficult. Hence the value of this work in which Fr Hallier helps us to discover and love Aelred, with particular reference to his teaching on monastic formation, and then to penetrate with him into this Cistercian's interior life, which had its primary setting in the concrete milieu in which he lived—and how very real that was!

Finally the doctrinal themes in which his soul found its food as well as its expression are elaborated and illustrated by apt quotations from his own writings.

Two features in particular distinguish this work and the service it can render to the reader. In the first place one cannot but admire the importance that is rightly given to terminology. How many treasures are waiting to be found in these writers if only we pay attention to the words they were fond of using! For they did not use these words haphazardly; even if, and we may say especially if, they were not aware of the similarity between their terminology and that of their predecessors and contemporaries, their very use of these terms reveals at once their sources and their originality. The words underlined so often throughout this book (the analytic index of them is a valuable feature of the work) are the common property of primitive monasticism and of St Bernard and his contemporaries. But so often each of the latter succeeded in enriching these words with some special nuance. The consistency they showed in using them bears witness to the unity of thought which imparts to their spiritual message its particular value and fruitfulness. When, with the help of instructive comparisons, we have grasped the meaning of some key word, this will then frequently suffice to cast light on an entire passage. When the full meaning of such a word has been comprehended, we shall find delight in recognizing it in other contexts, discovering echoes of it, enjoying all its overtones. A study on St Aelred can never dispense us from reading Aelred himself, but it can give us a taste for him, which, in its turn, will guide our reading. It serves to introduce us to Aelred's writings, prepare our minds for them and leave us to enjoy their beauty.

In the second place we appreciate how deserving these monastic writers are of serious study. Their works do not merely stir the reader piously (in the restricted and impoverished sense usually given to the word *pious*), without providing solid food for the mind. Fr Hallier proves from this monastic writer, who is so typical of them all, that they possess an authentic doctrine on the mystery of the monastic life with all its dogmatic and moral implications. Aelred is a theologian, and we shall not grasp the full significance of his teaching if we do not approach him from a theological viewpoint. The reader must not rest content with a superficial reading which would furnish him with moral exhortations, arouse the emotions perhaps, but which would fail to give the *raison d'être* for the monastic way of life. These Fathers must needs be read carefully, closely, constantly; such a reading will be a true study, in the best sense of the word *studium*. The wealth of religious experience and thought with which we will be put in contact will amply repay the effort expended. Fr Hallier has delved beneath the literary expression to discover the foundations and motives that explain and justify his full synthesis, the elements of which are to be found scattered through the whole of Aelred's works.

This book teaches us to read one of the witnesses of medieval patristic theology, which is not essentially different from the ancient patristic theology. In both, the writings are the expression of minds totally steeped in holy Scripture, so thoroughly had the Church's tradition brought the Word of God into the lives of monks and faithful in those ages. Today when we are striving to investigate and clarify every aspect of the message contained in the sources of Christianity, may we not believe that our age is continuing in the line of the ancient and medieval patristic theology; or that we are even standing on the threshold of—not a new patristic theology, since such must be essentially traditional—but a renewed patristic theology, a theology that is again a thing of the present, handed on and adapted to our contemporaries? All those who contribute to this renewal have a claim on our gratitude. Those who translated Fr Hallier's book—its richness of nuance made it no easy task—those who make its publication possible, all serve not only the cause of monasticism, which today is in full flood of development, but the cause of the Church which is unaging.

Jean Leclercq OSB

B

INTRODUCTION

AELRED OF RIEVAULX AND THE GROWTH OF THE CISTERCIAN ORDER IN ENGLAND IN THE TWELFTH CENTURY

I

The twelfth century was, from many points of view, an age of renewal.[1] In his own sphere and in his own way, Aelred of Rievaulx is as thoroughly typical of that amazing century as are his great contemporaries Hugh of St Victor, Peter Lombard, Abelard or St Bernard. By birth and monastic profession he had roots in Northumbria, which at that period was a cluster of counties on the rather shaky border between England and Scotland. Entering the Order of Cîteaux in the first flush of its expansion, Aelred caught there the pulsation of reform, always somewhat revolutionary, and breathed the air of self-assurance that surrounds every movement that has made a good beginning. Right from the noviceship of his monastic life he came under the influence of the most outstanding monk of his time, St Bernard. As abbot he was to achieve such greatness and influence in his Order and in his own country that his fellow countrymen could justly and not a little proudly hail him as the "Bernard of the North."[2]

1. Cf. C. H. Haskins, *The Renaissance of the Twelfth Century*, Cambridge, 1927; G. Pare, A. Brunet, P. Tremblay, *La Renaissance du XIIᵉ siècle, les écoles et l'enseignement*, Paris, 1933. For the economic renaissance see L. Halphen, *L'essor de l'Europe (XI-XIIIᵉ siècles)*, Paris, 1932.

2. Cf. D. Knowles, *The Monastic Order in England*, p. 240. Matthew, Cantor of Rievaulx, sings Aelred's praises by comparing him to St Bernard: *dulcedo fuit monachorum... similis Bernardo. Bernardo prope par... par ordo, par pietatis amor* (Migne, P. L. 195, col. 208).

With Aelred we have been more fortunate than with many other medieval writers, who are known to us solely by the writings they have left us: he had a biographer in the person of one of his closest disciples. The Abbot of Rievaulx had scarcely departed this life when one of his monks, Walter Daniel, began to write the life of the man who had been his superior and friend for seventeen years.[3] Of an impulsive and excitable temperament, Walter had marked preferences, and his omissions are significant. Of an intellectual bent, he showed little taste for administration or the material running of a great abbey. Typical of his time, he believed that it was the business of the hagiographer to scatter broadcast the aura of the miraculous. Aelred's companionship had delighted him, doubtless because of the high-mindedness he admired in his Abbot, but also, perhaps, because of the understanding shown him by this superior capable of adapting himself to all sorts of characters, be they as odd and singular as Walter's own. Moreover, it seems that these two men were complementary to each other in more than one respect. The fact is that Master Walter, as he was styled at Rievaulx,[4] was one of Aelred's intimate friends, especially towards the end of his life. The *Vita Ailredi*, for all the defects of author and work, stands as a valuable testimony of the interior life of St Aelred, his mentality as father and leader of his monks, and "the unique atmosphere he created around himself" at Rievaulx.[5] This record, at least in its authentic original, escaped the attention of historians for a long time.[6] We are indebted to Sir Maurice Powicke for an admirable

3. *Vita*, p. 40.   4. Cf. F. M. Powicke, *Vita*, Introduction, p. xiv.

5. Cf. D. Knowles, *op. cit.*, p. 645.

6. Until 1901 the only Life of Aelred which we possessed was to be found in the *Sanctilogium Angliae* of John of Tynemouth (fourteenth century), who had made use of Walter Daniel's MS. This Life was reproduced by Capgrave in his collection of the Lives of English Saints which Wynkyn de Worde printed in 1516. Bollandus in 1643 reprinted it in his first volume of the *Acta Sanctorum*, under the date 12 January. Republishing the *Nova Legenda Angliae* in 1901, C. Horstmann added in an appendix a longer version of the *Vita Aelredi* from the Bodleian MS. Bodley 240. F. M. Powicke showed, in 1922, that the common source of the two versions is the MS. of Walter Daniel.

edition of the *Vita*.[7] The holy Abbot's soul is mirrored in many of the pages of this Life, written in Rievaulx by a learned monk, who had been an observant eye-witness of his life. It must, however, be read with caution. The reader will need to be discerning to detect the traits, sometimes opportunely naive, sometimes deliberately affected, which reveal Walter's soul more often than Aelred's.

Aelred was born in 1110 at Hexham into a priestly family. It was a time of transition when clerical celibacy still admitted many exceptions. His father, Eilaf, enjoyed a well-merited reputation. Educated himself, he saw that his son received a sound education at the priories of Hexham and Durham.[8] Some years later the youth was in the service of King David I of Scotland (1124–1153), but it is not clear precisely when or in what circumstances he was received at Court.[9] For two or three years he held there the office of seneschal or high steward.[10] In later years he spoke of this period of his life in so conventional a fashion as to leave us without a clue as to the real nature of his experiences at the time. We get the impression, however, that he was becoming increasingly more receptive to a supernatural call that was making itself heard ever more distinctly.[11] A journey to Yorkshire decided his vocation all at once for him. On the way back he came upon the monastery recently founded

7. F. M. Powicke, *Ailred of Rievaulx and his biographer Walter Daniel*, Manchester, 1922. *The Life of Ailred of Rievaulx* by Walter Daniel, London, 1950.

8. An account of the schools of this period and area is to be found in Leach, *Early Yorkshire Schools*, in *Record Series of the Yorkshire Archaeological Society*, vol. XXVII.

9. We can hardly admit the opinion of W. M. Ducey who claims that Aelred spent about a dozen years at the Court of Scotland (see "St Aelred of Rievaulx and the Speculum Caritatis" in *The Catholic Historical Review* 17 [1931] 310). F. M. Powicke is more cautious: "We cannot be sure how old Ailred was, nor how long he stayed with David" (*Vita*, Introduction, p. xxxix).

10. *Vita*, pp. 3–4: *Erat tamen cum eo echonomus domus regalis . . . videlicet mense regalis dapifer summus.*

11. *Vita* p. 10: *Concepit in mentem nichil in mundo monachis perfectius uiuere ad promissa capessenda celestia. . . . Interim ardor desiderii cor eius inuadit, mentem occupat, animum optinet.*

by the White Monks in the valley of the Rye and already much talked of. He paid it a visit, and, won over by grace, he returned the following day to stay.[12]

In this new abbey, under the guidance of monks from Clairvaux, Aelred was formed to the Cistercian life by means of the Scriptures and the Fathers—St Augustine in particular—by meditation and by the practice of the Rule of St Benedict. He gave himself with enthusiasm to these formative disciplines,[13] and indeed to such evident advantage that we find him master of novices at Rievaulx in 1142, then Abbot of Revesby from 1143 to 1147, and finally Abbot of Rievaulx from 1147 to 1167. During all these years he never ceased to be the spiritual guide for his monks, a work for which the gentleness of his character coupled with the warm, deep, radiant sympathy of his heart seemed to have made him specially suited.

Aelred's writings have a close connection with his office as abbot. In them he shows himself totally dedicated to the formation of his monks, having ever at heart to make them grow in charity.

The first of his works chronologically, and his finest, is the *Mirror of Charity* (*Speculum caritatis*), written in 1142–1143 at the request of St Bernard. It is a practical treatise on Christian and monastic perfection,[14] in which the young novice-master of Rievaulx expounds his teaching on the excellence, discernment and practice of charity, the motive force behind the return to God of the soul created in his image. Chapter 35 of the third book of the *Speculum* is a long, revised form of a short treatise on the scope and aim of monastic profession which, in the short form edited by Dom Wilmart, appears to have been composed prior to the rest of the work.

In *When Jesus Was Twelve* (*De Jesu puero duodenni*), 1153–1157, a meditation on the journey to the Temple when Jesus was twelve

12. *Vita*, pp. 14–15.
13. *Am.*, Prol., edit. Dubois, pp. 3–5.
14. Cf. Dom A. Le Bail, "Aelred", in *Dict. Spir.*, t. I, col. 228.

years old, Aelred gives us, besides a charming and moving meditation on the actual event, an allegorical interpretation of it, which
sees in the episode a symbol of the Church's destiny and that of the
Synagogue, and a moral commentary in which the physical
growth of Christ is proposed as the exemplar and efficient cause of
our spiritual progress.[15]

On Spiritual Friendship (*De spirituali amicitia*), a little later—1160
approximately—is "the most eloquent and elegant of Aelred's
writings. It is the diary of his personal friendships, but he also takes
occasion to lay down the moral conditions for friendship between
Christians, thus perfecting in his own way the pagan philosopher
Cicero."[16]

A letter to his sister (*De institutione inclusarum*), 1160–1162, com-
posed at her request, is more than a mere rule of life for recluses.
Besides some vivid passages on the morals of his day, Aelred gives
autobiographical pictures that are reminiscent of St Augustine's
Confessions, and some modern-looking meditations on the life of
Christ.

Sermones de oneribus, 1158–1163, are, for the most part, a moral
commentary on chapters 13 to 16 of the Book of Isaiah, and treat
of the obstacles which the world, the devil and the concupiscence
of the flesh set up against the coming of Christ into the soul.

In his *Sermones de tempore et de sanctis* Aelred explains the meaning
of the liturgical mysteries and brings out their power to sanctify.

The *Pastoral Prayer* (*Oratio pastoralis*) is a "confession" that
reveals the soul of the Abbot of Rievaulx, and a prayer for those
entrusted to his care.

Aelred's final work, which remained unfinished, is a treatise *De
anima* which explained the anthropological foundation of his
doctrine on charity.

In addition to these spiritual writings there is a collection of

15. In 1958 Dom A. Hoste published a critical edition: Aelred de Rievaulx,
Quand Jésus eut douze ans, French translation by J. Dubois, Paris.
16. Dom A. Le Bail, *art. cit.*, col. 228.

historical works which do not directly serve our purpose. We merely note how significant is this side of Aelred's intellectual activity, which made of him one of the promoters of "the historical revival that is one of the glories of twelfth-century monasticism and bears comparison with any efflorescence of scholasticism . . . "[17]

2

The rapidity with which the Order of Cîteaux spread in England is most striking. It was not, indeed, the sole religious event of that period when the Christian renewal, set on foot in the previous century, was then producing such fruitful results, but it does appear as the most significant. It must be admitted that the time was favorable for this expansion. The society in which Aelred lived was not marked by the rivalry between the Normans and the Saxons subsequent to the Conquest; in Northumbria especially they lived side by side more peaceably than elsewhere.[18] Still less would it be correct to imagine that at this period there existed that racial conflict between the English and the Scots which was later to become so bitter and persistent. The Battle of the Standard, narrated by Aelred himself,[19] is to be seen as a feudal rather than a racial clash. But the world of that time was remarkable because it was in full ferment: demographic growth, commercial production, social emancipation, intellectual renaissance were all so many signs of a deep-reaching change; while a unique religious vitality was manifesting itself in the pursuit of order and authenticity.[20]

17. M.-D. Chenu, "Culture et théologie à Jumièges après l'ère féodale" in *Jumièges,* t. II, p. 781. See also Dom J. Leclercq, *The Love of Learning and the Desire for God.*

18. Cf. F. M. Powicke, *Vita,* Introduction, pp. xii and xliii.

19. P. L. 195, col. 702–12.

20. Cf. Ch. Dereine, "Vie commune, Règle de Saint Augustin et chanoines réguliers au XIᵉ siècle" in *Rev. Hist. Eccl.* 41 (1946) 365–406. "Les origines de Prémontré" in *Rev. Hist. Eccl.* 42 (1947) 352–98. "Odon de Tournai et la crise du cénobitisme au XIᵉ siècle" in *Rev. MA. Lat.* 4 (1948) 137–54. "Le premier Ordo de Prémontré" in *Rev. Bén.* 58 (1948) 84–92.

Such was the society, full of expectancy and relatively untrammeled, upon which Cîteaux burst with its dynamic freshness and its uncompromising demands, but with, in addition, an economic system peculiarly suited to the possibilities and needs of the time. And Cîteaux proved to be a success. Nothing gives a better idea of this success than the facts and figures. We shall consider only the quarter of a century from 1128, date of the first foundation. Waverley, to 1153, the year of St Bernard's death. There are two reasons for limiting ourselves to this period: first because this is *the* period of rapid expansion, and secondly because it was during this time that Aelred himself entered the Cistercian movement and received his formation in it. During these twenty-five years England witnessed the erection of fifty-eight Cistercian abbeys all over her land, in its valleys and glades.[21] Clairvaux, already the mother of sixteen daughter-houses, adopted Fountains, which in turn gave birth to thirteen daughters. Morimond had only one dependent monastery in England at this time. Savigny, which had been affiliated to the Order of Cîteaux in 1147, had fifteen daughter-houses in 1153 and L'Aumône thirteen. This golden age reached its peak in 1147—the year Aelred was elected Abbot of Rievaulx and a Cistercian became Archbishop of York—when seven new foundations were made within a few months. For various reasons the expansion was notably arrested from 1153 onwards. Before that date it had gone on at the rate of two or three foundations each year, but within the next sixty-four years only seven new abbeys were established.

The reasons for the phenomenal success recorded until the time of St Bernard's death are not at once apparent; events in religious history are due to the interplay of many causes, both natural and supernatural, whose very complexity makes it impossible to dis-

21. This includes the Savigniac family, affiliated to Cîteaux in 1147, the first English house of which, Furness (1123), existed before Waverley (1128), a foundation of L'Aumône.

tinguish the extent of their respective influences. So, rather than attempt to explain this extraordinary success and attraction, it seems preferable to illustrate it by examples, which bear witness to the spreading influence of Rievaulx from its foundation. Furthermore, these examples will give some indication of the spiritual values which the new monastic ideal stood for and the magnetic pull it had on men like Aelred, who were eager for perfection.

Scarcely had the White Monks settled in Yorkshire than their presence precipitated, if it did not provoke, a crisis in the great Benedictine abbey of St Mary at York.[22] The sight of these faithful observers of the Rule of St Benedict suddenly and sharply brought home to several of the York monks their own position "far from the Rule of their profession," at any rate, very far from the perfection which, to their mind, the Cistercian observance represented.[23] Ashamed of their mediocrity, a party was formed of which the prior became the leader. In consternation the aged abbot vainly tried to dissuade them from their purpose of reform. Conscious of their obligations, convinced of their laxity and fired with the desire to be faithful to their vows, they remained unmoved and appealed to the Archbishop,[24] who sided with them and promised his support. On an appointed day, he arrived at the monastery "in a spirit of gentleness and peace," but the abbot, surrounded by his adherents, refused all parley. Consequently Archbishop Thurstan put the abbey under interdict, and finally withdrew, taking with him the thirteen appellants whom he took under his protection and settled on his estates. This was the cradle of the famous Abbey of Fountains,

22. The account of this crisis, which resulted in the foundation of Fountains, has come down to us from two distinct sources: the narrative of the monk Serlo and the letter of Archbishop Thurstan. These two documents have been published by W. Dugdale in the *Monasticon Anglicanum*, t. V, pp. 292–97.

23. *Monasticon* . . . V, p. 292: *longe tamen citra praeceptum regulae, citra votum professionis suae, longe citra perfectionem Cisterciensis disciplinae.*

24. *Monasticon* . . . V, p. 293: *Ostendit ei pondus professionis, vivendi remissionem, conscientiae stimulum, proficiendi desiderium, nec posse rem ad effectum produci nisi episcopalis auctoritas inveniat.*

which Clairvaux subsequently adopted at the request of the founders. These pioneers, who had fallen under the spell of Cîteaux, were certainly men of no mediocre stamp: among them were seven future Cistercian abbots.

The same attraction made itself felt among the Canons Regular and gained an excellent vocation for the Cistercians. At the court of Scotland the young Waldef had been Aelred's friend and companion. Drawn to the religious life, he became a Canon Regular at Nostell and was elected Prior of Kirkham, not far from Rievaulx, about the time when his friend became a monk of that abbey. And then Waldef too was won over and determined to become a Cistercian, much to the displeasure of his confrères, who vented their spleen against the deserter who had fled to Rievaulx. Their anger was increased by the fact that his departure set up a division in the community and caused several others to express a desire to embrace the observance of Cîteaux.[25] Waldef, for a while repelled and depressed by the austerity of the Cistercian discipline, weathered the crisis, and later became Abbot of Melrose. This saintly man of exquisite refinement and Aelred were knit together by an enduring bond of friendship.

These two incidents, chosen from among many, demonstrate the influence exerted by Rievaulx right from the early years of its foundation. This abbey was the chief center of propagation of the Cistercians in the north of England and Scotland. The community increased with remarkable rapidity: from twenty-five monks in 1132, the number jumped to three hundred in 1142, and at the end of his life Aelred found himself responsible for six hundred and fifty

---

25. A short treatise by Aelred, a *disputatio* on monastic profession, published by A. Wilmart in *Rev. Asc. Myst.* 23 (1947) 259–73, seems to have been one result of this incident or others of a similar kind, which were neither rare nor irenical, especially when St Bernard intervened with his spirited conviction. See Vacandard, *Vie de saint Bernard,* t. I, pp. 186ff. A. Dimier, "Saint Bernard et le droit en matière de Transitus" in *Rev. Mabillon* 43 (1953) 48–82. Ph. Delhaye, "Saint Bernard de Clairvaux et Philippe de Harveng" in *Bulletin de la Soc. hist. et archéol. de Langres* 12 (1953) 129–38.

souls.[26] The monastery had quickly to send forth swarms and in a few years founded five daughter-houses, which in their turn multiplied still more. Rievaulx always maintained its magnetic power of attraction. In the first place, it had—so we are told by one of its monks—a charming site and seemed destined to become a "paradise."[27] The example of the monks roused the curiosity of those who observed them and stirred up a desire for a more God-centered life. This had been Aelred's own experience on seeing the monastery.[28] When he became the head and heart of this abbey, his most cherished desire was to make charity reign in it. Aelred's proper setting is Rievaulx; there he has to be seen living, not in solitude and tranquil recollection, nor in the pleasant company of a few select friends, but busy and ever eager to be at the service of those whose care he had undertaken. He must have been a shrewd administrator: he was a successful one. Under his guidance, Rievaulx prospered. In spite of worries involved in running a great monastery, and for all his genius for making friends and his healthy interest in the events of his day, Aelred succeeded in preserving his peace of mind. If he was not another St Bernard always on the road in the service of the Church, he was yet obliged, too often for his own liking, to undertake long journeys to attend to the interests of his daughter-houses. He appears to have been one of the most engaging and influential figures in the civil and religious society of his day.[29] Nevertheless Aelred's gifts of mind and heart did not find their finest expression in this domain; his genius is to be sought, not in the influence he wielded on the political and ecclesiastical events of his age, but in the more hidden and more difficult art of instructing and guiding his monks at Rievaulx on the path that leads to God.

---

26. *Vita*, p. 38, and n. 2. See also D. Knowles, *The Monastic Order* . . . , p. 258.
27. *Vita*, p. 12.
28. *Vita*, p. 13: "O, how greatly do I desire, how ardently I thirst for the sight of them, and to see for myself what you have told me about that happy place."
29. Cf. Powicke, *Vita*, Introduction, p. lxii.

In the eyes of historians of the Church in England, Aelred will always be the typical abbot,[30] head of a great monastery, mindful of his temporal and spiritual responsibilities, skilled in business affairs, but above all father of his monks and their master in the way of salvation. He devoted himself to their spiritual formation with the patient gentleness of manner that was characteristic of him, and with the love that inspired his whole *Pastoral Prayer:* "Lord, need I tell you my heart's longing? All you have given me, your servant, let it all, I pray, be theirs, be spent entirely on their behalf; not to mention how gladly I will spend myself on their behalf."[31]

Dedicated to the guidance of souls during almost his entire religious life, Aelred constantly pondered the meaning of the cenobitic life, and was a confirmed upholder of Cistercian observances.[32] He felt that his business was first and foremost to form and teach his monks.[33] This fact does not always appear to have been sufficiently noted, and yet it stands out prominently when we study his works. This pre-eminent quality of his has been hallowed by tradition, for the Abbot of Rievaulx is remembered as a guide of monks in their search for God. His *Mirror of Charity*, very soon summarized in, or more correctly converted into, a *Compendium*,[34] was read in the monasteries of the Middle Ages. His treatise *On Spiritual Friendship* was quickly paid the compliment of being plagiarized.[35] The letter to his recluse sister was extensively studied

30. Cf. Dom Pedrick, "Some Reflections on St Ailred of Rievaulx" in *Buckfast Abbey Chronicle* 14 (1944) 10.

31. *O. Past.* in A. Wilmart, *Auteurs spirituels et textes dévots du Moyen Age latin*, Paris, 1932, p. 294 (7).

32. This was Aelred's purpose in his "Court traité sur l'éntendue et le but de la profession monastique," published by A. Wilmart in *Rev. Asc. Myst.* 23 (1947) 259–73.

33. Cf. C. Hontoir, in *Collectanea O.C.R.* 1 (1934) 244.

34. Certainly in Clairvaux as early as the twelfth century. See A. Wilmart in *Rev. Asc. Myst.* 14 (1933) 429.

35. Cf. J. Dubois, *L'Amitié spirituelle*, Introduction, p. xcvi. Also E. Vansteenberghe, "Deux théoriciens de l'amitié au XIIe siècle" in *Rev. Sc. Rel.* 12 (1932) 572–88.

by monks and hermits,[36] but it was then attributed to St Augustine, and his *When Jesus Was Twelve* to St Bernard. Many other facts could be cited to prove Aelred's influence on Christian spirituality, especially in monastic circles.[37] Not that he was an innovator; on the contrary, his desire was to be fully in accord with tradition. Actually he took the elements of his doctrine from his predecessors or contemporaries: we have only to think of St Augustine and St Bernard. But the skill with which he assimilated the quintessence of monastic tradition, grasped and expressed the spirit of primitive Cîteaux, and added to these a charm and attractiveness peculiarly his own, cannot but compel our admiration. In his writings he deftly conjures up for us the Cistercian world of Rievaulx and makes it live in a most realistic way: "There are few medieval writings from which so much vivid material on the life of the cloister can be gleaned through anecdotes."[38]

Seen thus in the monastic setting which molded him and of which he became one of the most typical representatives, Aelred of Rievaulx will reveal himself for what he is—a master of the spiritual life who teaches his disciples lessons that are new and yet old. He teaches them the Word of God, but with the eloquence of a man

36. It was at that time attributed to St Augustine. See C. H. Talbot in *Analecta S.O.C.* 3–4 (1951) 169–70; also F. M. Powicke, *Vita*, Introduction, p. xcix. Ludolph the Carthusian makes extensive use of Aelred's little treatise in his *Vita Christi* but ascribes it to St Anselm.

37. The inventory, as yet incomplete, of MSS. in the English Cistercian abbeys shows the influence of Aelred's works on these monasteries. Cf. C. R. Cheney, "Les bibliothèques cisterciennes en Angleterre au XIIᵉ siècle" in *Mélanges saint Bernard,* Dijon, 1953, p. 379. M. Viller (*Rev. Asc. Myst.* 3 [1927] 78–79) regards Aelred as a precursor of the teaching on mental prayer. A.Wilmart claims that Gerard of Liège borrowed from Aelred; cf. *Analecta Reginensia* (*Studi e Testi* 59), Rome, 1933, p. 204, n. 3. Aelred's writings were held in high esteem by the Maurists. The Cistercian Dom Jean de Lannoy could write to Dom Luke of Achery: "You know that everything this holy Abbot wrote is excellent" (from a letter of 16 February 1673, published in the *Rev. Mabillon* 9 [1913] 225). See also another letter in the same review, 10 (1914–20) 135.

38. L. Bouyer, *The Cistercian Heritage* (translated by Elizabeth A. Livingstone), p. 132.

who has himself tasted its delight.[39] In his school we are put in contact with a true theology,[40] an *intellectus fidei* which is nourished by assiduous reading of Scripture and has a sacred regard for tradition. But—and here we sense the same concern for truth—this theology does not allow the study of the Word of the living God to be divorced from life, the monastic way of life which is neither more nor less than a seeking of God. In the *school of Christ* theological reflection is the prelude to spiritual experience.[41]

Our aim in this study is to portray Aelred as a master of the science of souls, to consider the witness he bore as a spiritual man and to outline the general principles of his theology which is the inspiration of a monastic way of life.

39. *S. Ined.*, p. 106: *Solus potest eructare qui novit gustare.* As in the case of St Bernard, this idea is frequently expressed by Aelred.

40. Dom J. Leclercq has rendered an outstanding service by showing, from their own writings, that the medieval monks are also theologians. See *The Love of Learning and the Desire of God*, New York, 1961. And by the same author: "Saint Bernard et la théologie monastique du XIIe siècle" in *Saint Bernard Théologien (Analecta S.O.C.* 9 [1953] 7–23).

41. *Jesu*, P. L. 184, col. 867b: *Et haec dicta pro modulo experientiae nostrae. S. Oner.* XIV, 418b: *Insta opportune, importune, ut contempleris faciem ejus, ut descendat ad te, vel te trahat ad se, ut gustes quam dulcis est, et quam mitis et misericors experiaris.*

PART ONE

MAN AND GOD

CHAPTER ONE

MAN THE IMAGE OF GOD

" THE spiritual teaching of the Cistercians of the twelfth and thirteenth centuries was not regarded as complete without a treatise *De anima*. Whether composed explicitly as a treatise, or touched on as occasion offered throughout their works, their teaching on this subject was the keystone of their doctrine on the sanctification of man."[1] It has sometimes been thought that the interest in psychology displayed by these monks was the result of the training they had received before entering the cloister.[2] But Aelred's case would appear to give the lie to such an assertion. His formation was acquired chiefly in the monastery, and he undertook his treatise *De anima* only at the end of his life, and in fact he left it unfinished. To his way of thinking, this treatise was the necessary complement of the doctrinal synthesis he had worked out, practiced and taught his monks during the course of his monastic life. Based on psychology, his doctrine was devised to lead the soul to the heights of the spiritual life.[3]

Created in God's Image

His doctrine begins with a study of anthropology, where no doubt he occasionally dwelt on the fanciful anatomy the "physicians" of

1. A. LeBail in *Dict. Spir.* 1 (1937) col. 1472. See also A. Squire in *Life of the Spirit* 7 (1952) 118–19.

2. This may perhaps be true of Alcher of Clairvaux who displays a particular flair for medicine and the natural sciences, although there are scarcely any details about his *curriculum vitae*.

3. Cf. C. H. Talbot, Introduction to the treatise *De Anima*, p. 27.

his time were so fond of,[4] but where his primary purpose was, following St Augustine, to depict the actual state of man, created by God but distorted by the wrong use of his liberty. This science of man is not the product of reasoning alone but is a theocentric anthropology that finds the origin and end of man in God: "God . . . the existence of whatever is, the life of whatever lives, the wisdom of all the wise."[5] It is to Revelation, in fact, we must look to learn how God considers his highest earthly creature. The key to the meaning of man is to be found in the text of Genesis: "let us make man in our image and in the likeness of ourselves,"[6] the creative Word of God that made man what he is and established his value solely on his relationship to God. The human soul is "the child of God" (Acts 17:28–29), not in the sense that it is "of his unique nature and substance," but that "created in his image . . . it is capable of participation in his wisdom and blessedness."[7] Therein lies the source of all our dignity. This doctrine of man as the image of God brings us to the core of Aelred's teaching,[8] and it is important to emphasize right at the start that this is a distinctly traditional line of thought.

In recent years the importance of the doctrine of the image, one of the basic themes of religious thought, has been brought out in some excellent studies, which attempt to explain man's enigma in terms of his relation to the Creator.[9] It is quite inadequate simply to say that the Fathers were influenced on this point, as on many others, by Platonism. The influence must be traced beyond hellen-

---

4. The physiological notions in Aelred's works are much less fanciful than in the *Physics* of William of Saint-Thierry.

5. It is curious to note that this opening passage of Sermon I *De Oneribus*, P.L. 195, col. 363b, is borrowed almost literally from Pseudo-Dionysius, *Hierarchia Celestis* IV, 1.

6. Gen 1:26. Cf. *Spec.* I, 3, 507d; I, 4, 509a. *S. Oner.* VII, 391b.

7. *Spec.* I, 8, 512d.

8. Cf. Dom Pedrick, *Sancti Ailredi de caritate doctrina, Excerpta*, p. 59.

9. A synthesis of the doctrine of the image is to be found in P. Th. Camelot, "La théologie de l'image de Dieu" in *Rev. Sc. Phil. Théol.* 40 (1956) 443–71.

istic culture to the earlier and obscurer sources upon which this culture itself drew. With many variations, depending on the cultural context or the immediate purpose of their writings, the Christian writers of the first centuries almost without exception spoke of man as the image of God. Even if they were following a philosophical and religious tradition in this, and if their sources were not exclusively Judeo-Christian, they certainly drew their inspiration from, and based their explanation on, the doctrine of the Book of Genesis (1:26), the sapiential books (Wis 2:23; 9:2-3) and St Paul. The revelation of the mystery of the Trinity and our divine adoption gives new depth and meaning to this notion of image.[10]

Throughout the Middle Ages this doctrine of the image remained a favorite theme and is to be found in all the outstanding Christian writers: John Scotus Erigenus, St Bernard, William of St Thierry, Hugh of Saint-Victor, etc. St. Thomas, too, took over this concept from tradition.[11]

As these few lines on this vast problem suggest, the task of tracing the sources of St Aelred's teaching on the image would prove very difficult. The influence of St Augustine is predominant, much more clearly discernible than it is in St Bernard or William of St Thierry, but this does not exclude the possibility of other sources. "Was there any Father, indeed any ecclesiastical writer who did not speak of the image, in detail or at least in passing?"[12] Instead of venturing on that interminable task, a wiser and more profitable course would be to explain Aelred's teaching on the subject of the image.

This concept may be referred to as the *natural image,* provided we understand the theological meaning Aelred gives to the word

10. See H. Crouzel, *Théologie de l'image de Dieu chez Origène,* Paris, 1955, pp. 57ff.

11. Cf. De Laugier de Beaurecueil, "L'homme image de Dieu selon saint Thomas d'Aquin" in *Etudes et recherches, Cahiers de Théol. et Phil.* 8 (1952) 45–82.

12. M. Standaert, "La doctrine de l'image chez saint Bernard" in *Eph. Theol. Lov.* 23 (1947) 125–27.

nature. According to his terminology, which is moreover the traditional one, the natural is generally not contrasted with the supernatural. It would certainly be incorrect to assert that this distinction, so evident in modern theology, was completely unknown to, or unused by, the writers of the twelfth century,[13] but they differed from us in their theological approach to the subject. They considered human nature as God had actually made it at the beginning of the history of salvation, that is, orientated towards God, the supernatural end, and destined to enjoy him in the beatific vision.[14]

But how and why is man the natural image of God? If Aelred admitted, as we shall see he did when we study the humanistic character of his work, that the body forms an integral part of human nature,[15] and if he did not underrate it, he did not, however, go so far as St Irenaeus who, with biblical literalness, did not exclude the body from the image doctrine.[16] Less Platonic, perhaps, than St Bernard, and less influenced than St Augustine by some of the obscure consequences of Manichean dualism, Aelred is nevertheless distinctly an heir of St Augustine's spiritualism. Man is the image of God through his soul, which by its very constitution shows forth the Trinity: indeed it *is* a created trinity, made up of three parts united in a single substance—memory, intellect and will.[17] With great accuracy Aelred emphasizes this one, and at the same time threefold, distinctive mark of the human soul. While he dis-

---

13. Ph. Delhaye, in *Rev. MA. Lat.* 3 (1947) 225–44, has clearly shown that Geoffroy of Saint-Victor (†1195) made an unambiguous distinction between nature and grace.

14. Cf. J. M. Déchanet, "Le 'natura sequi' chez Guillaume de Saint-Thierry" in *Collectanea O.C.R.* 7 (1940) 141–48; A. Fracheboud, "L'influence de saint Augustin sur le Cistercien Isaac de l'Etoile" in *Collectanea O.C.R.* 11 (1949) 9–11.

15. *Spec.* III, 22, 596a.

16. *Adv. Haer.* V, 6, 1.

17. *Spec.* I, 3, 507d; *S. Ined.*, p. 107; cf. *Anima,* p. 80.

tinguishes and combines them, the three faculties remain but one and the same soul.[18]

We must be particularly on our guard against believing *a priori* that Aelred borrowed this, among other things, in passing from St Augustine, for whom he had a special regard and whose writings he constantly read all through his life. We hope to show in fact that Aelred himself rethought this concept of the image and assimilated it with remarkable coherence into the unity of his doctrine. For the present it is enough to emphasize the fact that the Abbot of Rievaulx engrafted his idea of the image into the comprehensive concept of creation. All God's creatures, since they are divine participations, have within them, or more correctly, *are* three gifts of God: the nature, the form (*species*) and the use (*usus*).[19] The divine image in the case of man is not something added on to the soul but has an ontological relation to the *nature* or *essence* of the soul.[20]

Two consequences derive from this conception. If the image is such a constitutive element of the soul's nature, if it is essential to man's spiritual nature, then it cannot be destroyed. It can never be lost as long as the soul itself exists. It can be marred but not destroyed.[21] This ontological aspect of God's image in man, clarified by the distinction between the image and the likeness, is of immense importance in Aelred's spirituality.

The second consequence gives a still more wonderful insight into man's destiny. The image, rooted as it is in his very being, creates in him a *capacity*, a capacity for God, in the sense that his

18. *Anima*, p. 80, where we find reminiscences of St Augustine whom Aelred moreover quotes (*De Trinitate* X, 2, 18). Among St Bernard's disciples, Aelred shows himself, on this point, more faithful than the others to Bernard's teaching on the structure of the soul (Cf. E. von Ivanka, in *Saint Bernard Théologien,* p. 208).

19. *Spec.* I, 2, 506b.

20. *S. Ined.*, p. 108: *Imago que in homine rationali essentia naturaque consistit . . .; sic animam rationalem secundum naturam seu essentiam ad dei imaginem factam . . .* (the *sui* in the edited text is an obvious error; it should read *seu*).

21. *Spec.* I, 4, 508d. Cf. also 507b.

creation by God has made man capable of a blessedness to which he has absolutely no right and which consists in union with God by knowledge and love: "Only an intellect-endowed creature is capable of such blessedness as this. Created in the image of its Creator, it is able to cling to him, to him whose image it bears; this being the sole content of such a creature; as David puts it, I know no other content but clinging to God."[22] Our modern sensitiveness about theological precision need not be disturbed by the idea of a nature having a capacity for God. In the first place, Aelred, as we pointed out above, did not draw the distinction between the natural and the supernatural. It is therefore better to allow for this lack of determination than to force the doctrine into a structure that is foreign to it. Secondly Aelred clearly admits the unquestionable gratuitousness of this blessedness: union with God is his own gift; "of itself a creature simply cannot find happiness; it must receive it as a gift from the sovereignly blessed source of all the happiness of the blessed."[23] The capacity of which Aelred is here speaking is a certain spiritual affinity with God who is spirit: "Yes, the memory is capable, by participation, of eternity, the intellect of wisdom, the will of joy."[24] Finally he clearly states elsewhere that the soul cannot effectively participate in God unless he impresses the divine likeness on this image.[25]

St Irenaeus was doubtless the first of the Fathers to introduce into Christian theology the hellenistic distinction between image (*eikôn*) and likeness (*homoiôsis*). If he himself did not adduce the text of

---

22. A simple comparison of texts shows clearly that this doctrine is Augustinian:

Eo quippe ipso imago ejus est quo ejus CAPAX est, ejusque particeps esse potest; quod tam magnum bonum nisi per hoc quod IMAGO ejus est, non potest.
(St Augustine, *De Trinitate*, XIV, c. VIII, s. II)

Hujus beatitudinis sola rationalis creatura CAPAX est. Ipsa quippe ad imaginem sui Creatoris condita, idonea est illi adhaerere cujus est IMAGO.
(Aelred, *Speculum Caritatis*, I, c. III, col. 507d)

23. *Spec.* I, 3, 507d.   24. *Ibid.*   25. *S. Ined.*, p. 108.

Genesis (1:26) as a scriptural foundation in support of this distinction, others after him did so and a complete doctrinal thesis, in many ways very fruitful, was built on an exegesis that modern biblical scholars no longer accept.[26]

In Aelred's teaching, the distinction between the image and the likeness assumes a special importance that will be seen in the general structure of his doctrine. But because the terminology of medieval writers is not always a fixed constant, the meaning of certain key words must be determined in each case by the context. It is not strictly accurate to say, as Dom Pedrick does,[27] that the likeness always denotes the perfect image restored in the soul by grace. In the sermon *The Lord's Coming (De adventu Domini)*,[28] for instance, the expression "the likeness of God" means every trace of the divine likeness written in the very nature of creatures insofar as they are effects of God the Creator.[29] Elsewhere likeness is synonymous with image.[30] On the other hand, when it is used in conjunction with the notion of image, likeness expresses the idea of perfection,[31] a perfection that is added over and above (*superaddita*), that does not belong to the essence of the soul, that is gratuitous (*impressa per gratiam*).[32] This "supernatural" likeness restores the pristine beauty of the image and brings it into line with the divine exemplar, making it capable of connatural knowledge of him and of union with him. It will reach its full accomplishment only in heaven.[33] Now man's problem is precisely this—to recover the divine likeness he has lost.

26. In the *Jerusalem Bible* the following note to this verse of Genesis is given: "Likeness, by excluding the idea of equality, weakens the force of 'image'."

27. B. Pedrick, *S. Ailredi de caritate doctrina, Excerpta,* p. 25: *Similitudo significat* semper *imaginem* perfectam per gratiam *in animam impressam.*

28. Not yet published, it is true, when Dom Pedrick wrote his thesis.

29. *S. Ined.,* p. 34.

30. *Anima,* p. 67.

31. This idea of perfection is clearly evident in the traditional figure (used by Origen, Athanasius and Gregory of Nyssa) of the artist painting a picture. Aelred in his turn used this comparison: *S. Ined.,* p. 108. On the other hand, man, by sinning, lost the likeness, but the image remains: *Spec.* I, 4, 508d.

32. *S. Ined.,* p. 108; *S. Oner.,* 391c.   33. *Spec.* I, 5, 509b.

Withdrawal from God and Return to Him

If we are to understand properly the nature of the spiritual life, which Aelred always presents as a restoration or reparation—noting the particular significance of the prefix *re*[34]—not as a pure and simple ascent to God, we must consider the successive stages of the history of the fall and renovation, which Aelred makes the chief object of his monastic teaching, and in doing so follows faithfully the line traced out by St Benedict in the prologue of his Rule.[35] After considering man's dignity as he came forth from his Creator's hand and then the wilful deviation that caused his downfall, Aelred goes on to describe the wretchedness which the sinner knows by bitter experience until, taken up again by God, he is converted and turned back towards him through Christ the indispensable mediator. Man thus retraces the long journey of the prodigal son. While he is on the return road, *charity* by degrees sets everything in order anew in him.

Now, at the beginning of time, in a world where God's creatures were "good in their natures, fair in their forms, each conducing, according to its place in the scheme of things, to the beauty of the universe,"[36] God raised the human soul, born of his breath, to a unique dignity. In the midst of this universal harmony, man, lord of the material creation, was totally orientated towards God, his soul's focus and center of attraction: "Unwearingly man's memory held God; his intellect knew him unerringly; his will, undistracted,

---

34. *S. Ined.*, pp. 80 and 89. M. M. Lebreton, in *Rech. Théol. Anc. Méd.* 23 (1956) 13, remarks that this is a constant theme of twelfth-century preaching: "In the majority of sermons, redemption is considered under this aspect, and the elements of this recreation of the human race are enumerated in great detail."

35. ". . . that by the labor of obedience you may return to Him from whom you had departed by the sloth of disobedience" (*Rule of Saint Benedict,* Prologue, translation L. Doyle, Collegeville, Minnesota, Liturgical Press, 1948, p. 1).

36. *Spec.* I, 2, 506c.

enjoyed him by love."[37] For Adam it was the happiness that springs from peace: "Peace abode in his being . . . peace dwelt in his mind . . . in his will was peace."[38] Yet even in this state of blissful friendship with God, man had complete liberty of choice in his actions. "The gift of free choice made it possible for our First Parents, aided by God's grace, to love God faithfully, to enjoy remembering and knowing him, to be happy forever. On the other hand, it enabled him to turn his love to something less, that is, not merely to withdraw and cancel his loving of God, but to devote himself to wretchedness."[39] Indeed, as long as he remains in transit on earth, every creature remains mutable; this is one of his essential marks; without it, says Aelred, he would no longer need God and could neither advance nor go back.[40] Endowed with liberty, man has the power to consent to a lesser good and thereby estrange himself from the supreme Good. Wanting to be his own master without God,[41] he freely chose to turn away from him and in his search for happiness he actually selected a way that brought him ruin and unhappiness.

How did this withdrawal from God take place? Love is the pivot of Aelred's doctrine right from the beginning of man's history. His estrangement from God is mainly a matter of his *affectus*, that inclination of his towards an object conceived as good.[42] "How, you ask, have you gone away from me? Lord, it seems to me that it came about through the mind's affection, not by the motion of the feet."[43] Blinded by disordered self-love, man preferred a created good to the infinite Good. He made a deliberate choice, aware of what he was doing, for there is no sin without the reason coming into play.[44] So the withdrawal was the result of an act of the will on the part of the rational creature.[45] Man's godward alignment is altered

---

37. *S. Ined.*, p. 108.   38. *S. Ined.*, p. 101.   39. *Spec.* I, 4, 508b.
40. *S. Oner.* XVII, 431b-c. See also *Spec.* I, 13, 517b-c; I, 8, 512d.
41. *Spec.* I, 7, 512a.   42. *Spec.* III, 2, 587d.   43. *Spec.* I, 7, 512a.
44. *Spec.* III, 8, 584c-d.   45. *S. Oner.* XV, 424a.

precisely by this act of his will. Cupidity plunged him into wretchedness. Henceforth man is no longer to be seen in an Eden of happiness but has become a wanderer, far from his lost Paradise, in the land of unlikeness to which he has banished himself in turning away from God.

This expression, the land of unlikeness, has engaged the attention of several scholars for some years past and certain distinctions have gradually been established. "Originating with Plato and Plotinus . . . it was adopted by Christian writers such as Eusebius, St Athanasius and St Augustine, until we find it has become almost universal in the Middle Ages."[46] But, while the majority of these Christian authors associate the land of unlikeness with the far country in St Luke (15:13) and thus emphasize the notion of sin, St Bernard[47] differs from them in following the Platonic idea of the soul that is an alien on earth, an exile in the *topos tês anomoiotêtos*, in a land that is not its true country.

If St Bernard started a tradition on this point within the Order of Cîteaux,[48] it is interesting to discover whether Aelred subscribes to this tradition. Bernard's concept of the land of unlikeness seems to color the following passage in which Aelred suggests the idea of man, placed on earth, as an exile among the animals: "Each being occupies the place that suits it; for example, angels are in heaven, beasts on earth; men with their composite natures are in between, in a kind of half-way paradise. . . . Why should man complain over having, at present, to share the beasts' situation, when his carelessness in prosperity put him on a level with them, made him their like." But he immediately explains his comparison by adding that man's similarity to the beasts cannot be reduced to a question of situation but results from an internal condition of his: "When an intellectual soul loses its being like to God, though not its being in his image, its close likeness to unreasoning beasts is past all explaining."[49]

46. J. M. Déchanet, in *Saint Bernard Théologien*, p. 69.
47. *Ibid.*, p. 70.   48. *Ibid.*, p. 71.   49. *Spec.* I, 2, 506c–507b.

In other places the context helps to determine Aelred's notion of the land of unlikeness. The expression is associated with three other notions, namely the parable of the prodigal son, the movement of the withdrawal and return to God, and the fundamental idea of the image,[50] and these comparisons are particularly instructive. The prodigal son went astray in the land of unlikeness, learning by experience how destitute he was: "I, no other, am that prodigal. Selfishly I clung to my inheritance. Serve thee I would not. I went instead to the far-off country, the land of unlikeness."[51]

The soul loses its divine likeness when it turns away from God; hence withdrawing from God becomes synonymous with straying in the land of unlikeness: "How was the prodigal son able to go far from, able to come near to, him who is in every place? Can there be any country far from him beyond whom is nothing? No, the far country stands for unlikeness, while being like means being close at hand."[52] Man made in God's image and likeness can, by his own fault, not destroy, but mar the image by stripping it of the divine likeness. The examination of the idea of unlikeness, therefore, leads us to the central idea of the divine image in man: "The adopted son, created in the image and likeness of him . . . is able to go far away because he is able to lose the likeness, is able to return because he is able to regain it."[53]

In the passages quoted it is clear that Aelred connects the notion of unlikeness with the idea of sin, fall and estrangement from God. It is the country of sin where man, blinded by his self-love, has gone astray. While unlikeness is linked with the idea of perversion, and ultimately pride,[54] the likeness on the other hand is the country of *virtue*.[55] Likeness is a gift of God, unlikeness the effect of man's

---

50. On this theme col. 391 of sermon VII *De Oneribus* is particularly stimulating.

51. *Jesu*, P. L. 184, 852a; cf. *S. Oner.* VII, 391a.

52. *S. Oner.* VII, 391a.   53. *Ibid.*, 391b.   54. *Spec.* I, 4, 508b.

55. The word *virtus* is here used in the sense in which it is used by the Fathers : participation in the Virtue par excellence, the Word of God.

wickedness.[56] It is the harmful leaven of corruption, placed in us by sin and contaminating our nature.[57]

In figurative and vivid language, frequently borrowed from Scripture, Aelred describes this land of unlikeness as a place of misery and darkness, a place of horror and a land of want.[58] The context is always seen to be the same—sin and estrangement from God: the human soul has lost its pristine beauty and is compared to the brute beasts.[59] What of the divine image in the prodigal son who, in turning away from God, had become a sinner? Even in this far country where he is astray, the image of God remains in his soul.[60] The seal of the Trinity, imprinted in the substance of a rational being, cannot be destroyed without the nature itself being, at the same time, annihilated.[61] The sinful soul continues, therefore, to be the natural image of God, but this image is now defaced, "deformed," the form being the likeness of God.[62] Consequently the soul still retains its spiritual powers, but their operation is perverted because turned away from God, since the image has true likeness only when it is turned towards God and taken up with him: "Memory, consequently, persists, though liable to forgetfulness; intelligence, but subject to error; loving does also, if with a pronounced bent towards selfishness."[63]

Aelred repeatedly paints the picture of the spiritual wretchedness of fallen man, despoiled of the divine likeness. Man's sorry plight is indeed a constant theme of medieval theologians since the time of Gregory the Great.[64] A miserable lot, to be sure, is his who has gone astray, has left God, the beginning and end of his being: "Clinging

---

56. *S. Oner.* VII, 391c.   57. *S. Temp.* XII, 278d.   58. *Spec.* I, 7, 512a.

59. *Spec.* I, 26, 528c; I, 2, 507b. This is a traditional theme of patristic literature.

60. Cf. *supra*, p. 7.

61. *Spec.* I, 4, 508d.

62. *S. Ined.*, p. 34.

63. *Spec.* I, 4, 508d.

64. Cf. Gillet, *Introduction aux Morales sur Job* (*Sources chrétiennes*), pp. 16–18.

to God, and it only, spells full content for an intellectual creature, and, in its turn, withdrawal from him is the only misfortune."[65]

For the image there can be no neutral position in relation to its exemplar: either it must be happy with him or else wretched without him. No other alternative, no other state exists for the creature endowed with reason: "What more fit reward than beatitude for a free creature that has kept right? Is not wretchedness its due if it prove itself wicked?"[66] The soul desired blessedness but apart from God, and the actual result of this is that the soul now groans beneath a triple yoke: the yoke of sin, habit and unhappiness.[67] Thus abandoned to himself, man is now no longer any better than a harlot,[68] a wounded man lying half-dead by the wayside,[69] a rebel at variance simultaneously with God, the angels and the devil.[70] How true it is that his misery is great and manifold![71]

In God's plan this bitter experience is meant to be beneficial for man, to serve as the prelude to his conversion. In suffering and humiliation the wretched prodigal becomes aware of his exile, realizes his destitution and sees his deformation. It is the experience of his true destiny, but in reverse. His wretchedness and pain make him long for a restoration, God's gift indeed but one that corresponds to the aspirations of his whole being. The soul, gone astray, must needs learn to know itself;[72] it will then come to realize that something within it is clamoring; it suffers because it is torn apart interiorly. With the inmost depth of his soul divided, the sinner is in opposition to his true end and it is in vain that he seeks peace: "Pitiful, duped creature that staked all on joy unworthy of the

---

65. *Spec.* I, 4, 508b.   66. *Spec.* I, 2, 507a.   67. *S. Oner.* XIX, 442b.
68. *S. Oner.* XX, 446b.   69. *S. Ined.*, p. 101.   70. *S. Ined.*, p. 38.
71. *S. Ined.*, p. 71.

72. St Bernard and the Cistercians of the twelfth century laid great stress on the necessity of self-knowledge. E. Gilson in *The Mystical Theology of St Bernard*, p. 70, writes: "To know ourselves is essentially, in his view, to recognize that we are defaced images of God." Cf. C. H. Talbot, Introduction to *De Anima*, p. 24; C. Bodard in *Saint Bernard Théologien*, p. 28; J. M. Déchanet in *Cîteaux in de Nederlanden* 4 (1953) 297.

name . . . took wretchedness for its lot while keeping its longing for bliss, and so ever restless treads its chosen round of misery."[73]

But man remains God's image; his downfall is not irreparable. The Father is mindful of the prodigal son. We have now to examine the sinner's possibilities of restoration and the conditions of the conversion that opens up his return to God. If man, who is naturally mutable, has the power to choose a created good, the enjoyment of which is incompatible with the possession of the supreme Good, and as a result of this free choice, cut himself off from God, he likewise has the privilege, by God's grace, of returning to him.[74] Free will comes into play, then, in regard to evil as in regard to good; it is the *power of consent:* with grace to consent to good, or to consent to evil in spite of grace.

Here it is advisable to refer to the image concept in order to understand the possibility of man's return to God and his need for such a restoration. Every image has a dynamic tendency towards its exemplar. The tendency of the soul, God's image, towards him is something that belongs, as a characteristic property, to its nature; not to tend to him would be to deny its own highest good. Undoubtedly man endowed with liberty can determine the course of his life; but whatever course he takes, whether willingly consented to or only endured, the basic dynamic tendency of the divine image within him cannot be annihilated. If he turns away from God, he goes astray and contrary to his own nature, and so causes his own unhappiness; if he tends towards him, he finds his own fulfillment and his happiness besides. Man's whole problem lies therein, a problem that is worked out during his earthly life, that is, during the entire time allotted him to make his free choices.

Another law, a norm of every creature, forces itself upon the man astray in the land of unlikeness, and that is the law of *order*. The concept of order had a permanent influence upon medieval

73. *Spec.* I, 22, 526a.
74. *S. Oner.* VII, 391b.

thought.[75] From St Augustine to St Bernard[76] and St Thomas[77] it recurs as a constant factor and reveals itself equally in the theological *summae* as in the Gothic cathedrals, in the *Little Exordium* of Cîteaux[78] as in the *Divine Comedy* of Dante. Set in an Augustinian frame this universal law of things is enunciated by Aelred thus: "Every creature tends towards, seeks its place in, the scheme of things; it finds no rest save there."[79] All the exacting demands of this law of order continue to be felt in the land of unlikeness and create in the soul an unrest that cannot be appeased. God is and always will be the home of the soul that is his image. In him, and in him alone, will it find rest. As long as it has not returned to him, or at least begun to return by conversion, the soul experiences the pain of being torn asunder by forces tugging it in opposite directions.

The general notion of order, which is closely connected with the image notion, leads to the whole problem of beatitude. Every creature has its appointed end, which is its good, and it will find peace only in possessing this end. Man, God's image, attains his fulfillment only in God; if he turns away from him, the experience of his wretchedness and poverty only renders his need more acute, and the unhappy man, unable to lose his yearning for beatitude, simply goes on in a vicious circle, the vicious circle of the soul that is not at rest.[80] Thus everything conspires to urge the prodigal

75. Cf. M. Standaert, "La Théologie de l'image . . ." in *Eph. Theol. Lov.* 23 (1947) 71, and the bibliography given by this writer.

76. M. Standaert, "Le principe de l'ordination . . ." in *Collectanea O.C.R.* 8 (1946) 178–216, has shown that St Bernard was radically inclined to consider all things, including man and the spiritual life, from the viewpoint of the order already existing or to be established.

77. E. Gilson, *Introduction à l'étude de saint Augustin,* p. 168 and note.

78. Without stopping to consider the historicity of the document in question, we find in it a resolute determination to be faithful to the Rule and a concern for order which is very much in keeping with the spirit of the period. There is an English translation of the *Exordium* by R. Larkin in L. Lekai, *The White Monks* (Okauchee, Wisconsin, 1953) pp. 251–66.

79. *Spec.* I, 21, 524c. A few lines earlier the Augustinian idea of peace is suggested: *tranquillitas ordinis.* Cf. 524b.

80. *Spec.* I, 22, 526a.

D

son to return to the Father: the image retains its natural bent and tends towards its exemplar; the soul still keeps its power to choose, and the desire for happiness, never satisfied, makes its insistent appeal within it.

Conversion marks the radical change that takes place between the two opposite movements of the withdrawal from and the return to God. Assisted by grace the human person turns anew to God and wills him as its supreme end. This turning about can only be done by a free act of the will, a *consensus*,[81] which is an act of assent to a call from above and of consent to the image's tendency within. In taking this step the created spirit affirms its privilege "of either devoting itself to God or withdrawing from his service."[82] The withdrawal was a voluntary act and voluntary too must be the return. But while man can turn away from God by his own power, using his liberty, he cannot unaided extricate himself from his wretchedness; for this, divine help is absolutely necessary. Man freely made himself a sinner; "there is no sinning without willing." But his own will alone is not sufficient to make him justified again: "only grace lifts the will to holiness."[83] God alone can effect this change;[84] without his intervention we could not of ourselves retrace our steps back to him.

Through Christ

Man was unable, then, to set himself free. If his own wretchedness lay heavy upon him, still more oppressive was the tyranny of his

---

81. Through this *consensus* the divine likeness was lost: see *S. Oner.* XV, 424a. And it is by *consensus* that restoration must be brought about. This is a basic notion with these authors. Cf. Aelred, *Spec.* I, 10; St Bernard, P. L. 182, 1002c, 1003a; P. L. 183, 117c. See also A. Forest, "L'expérience du consentement selon Saint Bernard" in *Collect. O.C.R.* 18 (1956) 269–75.

82. *Spec.* I, 4, 508b.

83. *Spec.* I, 12, 516b; Cf. *S. Oner.* VII, 391c.

84. *S. Temp.* I, 216c.

enemy, the Devil. Adopting the same viewpoint as the Fathers, Aelred paints a dismal enough picture of the spiritual enslavement of the human race before the coming of the Messiah to redeem it. In all the details of this picture we catch a late reflection in the twelfth century of the theory of the so-called rights of the Devil. From the fall of Adam till the coming of Christ, the whole human race lay under the dominion of Satan.[85] There was no one to challenge his reign;[86] he arrogated to himself rights over fallen man,[87] and exercised a tyrannical control over him. This cruel Pharaoh[88] persecuted and oppressed all God's chosen friends, "using his wickedly acquired right, even in the case of the predestined."[89] From the North, the darksome and chilly land of his choice, he held sway over all the children of Pride and was at pains to disseminate Envy, Wrath and Lust.[90]

Who could dethrone him? The Devil was strong, but Christ was stronger.[91] God himself came to our rescue; in the person of his own Son the Almighty accomplished his distinctive work for us, that is, the work signified by his name, which, according to Aelred, is redolent of charity and mercy.[92] He showed his mercy towards the wretched creatures we are; "the miserable have a claim on God's merciful design."[93]

Christ, our Samson, the conqueror of the Devil and our Liberator, broke the bonds with which Satan had enchained mankind;[94] "the debt which burdened all our race has been paid; cancelled the deed, the decree which made us liable to our prime enemy's inveterate pride."[95] And so, by his power, this Solomon, our peacemaker, restored peace between men and God.[96] More than that, he gave back to man the divine gifts which were his patent of nobility at the dawn of his career. God had created Adam in godlike greatness,[97]

85. *S. Temp.* I, 214b.   86. *S. Oner.* XIX, 439a.   87. *S. Oner.* XXVI, 480c.
88. *Ibid.*   89. *Ibid.*   90. *S. Ined.*, p. 71.
91. *S. Ined.*, p. 96.   92. *S. Temp.* XII, 280d.   93. *Ibid.*, 281a.
94. *S. Ined.*, p. 96.   95. *Spec.* I, 5, 509b.
96. *S. Temp.* I, 212d ; *S. Ined.*, p. 38.   97. *S. Ined.*, p. 31.

but by his transgression man was reduced to, and held fast in, a state of degradation.[98] Christ came and restored the human race to its former dignity.[99]

The mysterious and moving economy of redemption reveals itself to us like this: the image of God, which had been disfigured in us, had to be restored to the divine likeness by him who does not merely bear God's image and likeness but is himself the Image who is the perfect likeness of the Father.[100] This restoration is adapted to our condition as beings whose destiny is worked out in time. The gradual repair of the ravages of sin is accomplished by efficacious means, sacraments by which Christ carries on in us the process of making us like to God: "The promises of Holy Scripture rectify the memory, the mystery of the Redemption restores the intellect, daily-growing love purifies one's affections."[101]

Christ is the one and only Way that will bring us to God. He comes from God; he came down that we may go back up with him and by him.[102] He becomes one of us in his human nature and did not hesitate to clothe himself with our debt to death and all its consequences,[103] to put on the skin garment of our lowly human condition.[104] Therefore we have to study carefully the incidents of his earthly life because the stages he passed through on his earthly journey are the pattern of our ascent to God: "His bodily growth is the exemplar of our spiritual progress to such an extent that what we read of his development is experienced, step by step, spiritually, by those who go steadily forward."[105]

Christ's humanity is our way to God; "there is no coming to the Father most high but by this way."[106] Anyone who thinks otherwise is deceived.[107] Our spiritual life must be a Christ-life, that is, it must be a life in Christ; even more than that, it means that Christ must

98. *S. Ined.,* p. 90.   99. *Ibid.*   100. *S. Oner.* VII, 391b.
101. *Spec.* I, 5, 509b.   102. *S. Temp.* XXI, 327d.   103. *S. Temp.* XII, 279a.
104. *S. Temp.* XXIII, 344d; 345a.   105. *Jesu,* P. L. 184, 856a
106. *S. Temp.* XXI, 327d.   107. *S. Temp.* XII, 282d.

live and grow and develop in us.[108] So an ever-deepening knowledge
of the Son of Mary goes hand in hand with our gradual advance-
ment towards God. In his own way and in his own time, the Holy
Spirit brings us from the knowledge of Christ in his human nature
to the revelation of Christ as a life-giving Spirit.[109] Then it is that
our mind receives a deeper understanding of the Scriptures. There
can be no transition from the letter to the spirit independently of
Christ.[110] Similarly each "Sabbath" of the soul, those moments of
peace and sweetness which mark our ascent to God, is connected
with a more intimate degree of knowledge of the Incarnate Word.[111]
The entire work of salvation centers on Christ. In a sense we can
never go beyond Christ since he is God. Aelred can, therefore,
summarize the way St Benedict himself followed and taught his
sons in this epigrammatic phrase: Through Christ to Christ.[112]

Man's problem can find no solution save in Christ. It is Christ
who, through his Spirit, transforms us bit by bit into the likeness
of God who is Love. He alone can effect in us that most sacred form
of charity, friendship.[113] "The beginning and end of all spiritual
friendship is Christ; its progress is Christ's doing."[114] Christ himself
is to be loved as the most intimate of friends.[115] No earthly love must
be allowed to compete with the love of Christ: "To him alone
belongs any love we have for anyone; by himself and for himself

---

108. *Jesu*, P. L. 184, 852d (Cf. Eph 4:13).

109. Such was the experience of St Gilbertine of whom Aelred spoke in
Sermon II *De Oneribus*: col. 371b : *Hac igitur luce perfusa ipsum Christum quem
prius noverat secundum carnem coepit j am secundum carnem non nosse; quia spiritus
ante faciem ejus Christus Jesus in ipsam eam induxerat veritatem.* Aelred here
applies this distinction to mystical experience. Elsewhere the knowledge
secundum spiritum means the beatific vision. See *S. Temp.* XVIII, 310c and 313b.

110. *S. Ined.*, p. 42. To effect the transition from the law to the Gospel, from
the letter to the spirit, from the Old Testament to the New, there is required
the power of the Lord's passion. See also *Jesu*, P. L. 184, 858; *S. Temp.* XXI,
328a.

111. *Spec.* III, 6, 583d.   112. *S. Temp.* VI, 245d.   113. *Spec.* III, 39, 619b.

114. *Am.*, 662c; ed. Dubois, p. 12.   115. *S. Temp.* I, 212b.

he claims chief place in our affection."[116] But we are to have no mistaken idea of this affective devotion towards Jesus, "so pleasant when present, so fair when seen, such a delight to embrace;"[117] as Aelred taught it, it is neither soft nor sentimental. He will have his monks to be, before all else, lovers of the Cross: "In Christ's Cross there is no room for softness, flabbiness, daintiness, for what flatters flesh and blood. Christians should take the Cross of Christ for their standard. . . . Our way of life is for us the Cross of Christ."[118]

While we are wayfarers on this earth we are constantly united to Christ. In all our struggles he cannot forsake us. Now in heaven he still lives with us by being able to feel for us; mindful of our sufferings, he is always ready to help us.[119] If we have much to suffer on earth, it is only so that we may share in the glory of the whole Christ. We are indeed the living stones, cut and chiseled, that one day will be carried up to heaven to become with the angels the Lord's throne on high.[120] When this throne is completed, Christ will appear with all his members united in the bond of charity.[121]

Through Mary

It would be impossible to treat Aelred's mariology at length here; nevertheless it cannot be passed over in silence.[122] But it is not easy to give a correct presentation of it. If we exaggerate its importance, we would be doing Aelred a disservice; if we consider it without reference to the central theme of man's return to God, we would present a false idea of his doctrine.

---

116. *Spec.* III, 38, 618a.
117. *Jesu,* P. L. 184, 855a.
118. *S. Temp.* IX, 263c–d.
119. *S. Ined.*, p. 31.
120. *Ibid.*, p. 32.
121. *Ibid.*
122. Cf. A. Agius, "Saint Aelred and Our Blessed Lady" in *Downside Review* 64 (1946) 32–38. In this article the author has assembled the chief mariological themes of the Abbot of Rievaulx and added a brief summary of them.

Mary is inseparable from Christ. Devotion to her is intimately bound up with devotion to Christ. Mary is the mother of our Savior: therefore she is our mother "owing to Christ's birth from her." "She is really our mother. Through her comes our birth, our rearing, our growth. . . . She, then, Christ's mother . . . is the mother of our redemption. . . . Our true birth is of her."[123]

As the new Eve she has a part to play in our redemption. The virtues that shine forth in her stand out in contrast to the vices that brought about our downfall.[124] Mary received such favor from God that she revoked the curse that lay on the world.[125] Considering the mother of our Redeemer in this way, we cannot fail to see her place in the mysteries of the liturgical cycle, and this is in accord with sound theology. Hence it is frequently suggested that the feast of the Annunciation is the first of all the feasts of the year, because it marks the beginning of our redemption.[126]

With this connection between our salvation and Mary's motherhood in mind, Aelred is fond of extolling the plenitude of grace with which she has been filled. Repeatedly he asserts that we all receive of her fullness and suggests that she has been appointed mediatrix of grace in our regard.[127] Mary, the bride, handmaid and mother of God,[128] is associated with the work of her Son and shares in our redemption. She begets us to a new life; "She is more truly our mother than the mother who bore our flesh."[129] Eve forfeited the earthly paradise; the monk who follows Mary will recover paradise which here on earth is the peace of the cloister.[130]

123. *S. Temp.* XX, 323. 124. *S. Ined.*, pp. 84–85.
125. *S. Temp.* XXI, 326d. 126. *S. Ined.*, pp. 77, 83, 89.
127. *S. Ined.*, p. 80: *Plena, utique, de cujus plenitudine nos omnes accepimus.* *Ibid.*, p. 90: *Vere plena, de cujus plenitudine nos omnes accepimus. Ibid.*, p. 139: *Utinam de plenitudine ejus accipiamus, ut simus illius gratie benedictionisque participes.* Aelred, thus, consistently applies Jn 1:16 to Mary, with, of course, the necessary theological distinctions. Mary's mediation is likewise suggested in this text in *S. Ined.*, p. 90: *Plena certe non solum sibi sed omni omnino creaturae.*
128. *S. Temp.* XX, 322d. 129. *Ibid.*, 323c.
130. *S. Ined.*, p. 88.

Conclusion

Man was created by God in unique dignity. Since his soul was an image like unto God, it felt itself drawn, by a natural impulse informed by grace, to live a life completely taken up with God in his memory, intellect and will. But this godward orientation was to be the result of a free, deliberate act;[131] other goods were capable of drawing man's affections and that is precisely what did happen. Acting under the impulse of blind love, the soul turned towards a good of the sense-perceptible order and in so doing turned away from God. It lost at that moment the divine likeness and it learned to know by experience its wretchedness in the land of unlikeness. There God in his mercy came seeking it. The Uncreated Image restored the created image by meriting for it the grace to be re-created in the divine likeness. Since then the man who follows or goes Christ's way is reorientated towards God. No doubt conversion, at least according to the ordinary laws of the plan of salvation, does not mean a total reordering: time and patient effort to advance a long and wearisome way are needed for this, but conversion is the beginning of that work of restoration which is accomplished progressively by Christ and by the Holy Spirit.[132]

Man's whole pursuit then, is to become once more like to God. The program of formation for the soul, that is, for God's image, is clear-cut—to tend to an ever truer and deeper likeness to him. But this immediately raises another fundamental question which we must answer if we would solve man's enigma: *what is God?*

After thus defining man as a distinctly theocentric being and describing the two contrary movements of his history, Aelred has now to give us some idea of the God who fulfills this need for union with him, implanted by him in his created image.

---

131. *Spec.* I, 4, 508b.   132. *S. Ined.*, p. 109.

CHAPTER TWO

GOD IS FRIENDSHIP

IN the preceding pages we outlined in summary fashion the main points of Aelred's anthropology and described the position of the rational creature to whom two alternatives were presented: either to consent to the natural impulse of the image and tend to God or, on the contrary, to assert its relative autonomy in respect of the Creator by choosing and claiming to find its fulfillment without God. Man did, in fact, deliberately go off into a far country where he lost the divine likeness. The divine imprint still continued to be stamped in his very being; he remained the image, but now a distorted image, wretched because despoiled.[1]

Man is God's image: here we have the fundamental concept and the dogmatic-psychological foundation of Aelred's doctrine. The Abbot of Rievaulx cannot conceive man except in relation to God, and all his dignity has its origin in this privileged relationship to his Creator. If man's essential definition, therefore, is derived from this relationship to another Being, the study of the image must lead us to study the divine Exemplar. An accurate knowledge of the mystery of man cannot be obtained without considering the mystery of God. So having explained the central idea of Aelred's anthropology, we have now to try to understand the apex of his theology. In doing this we shall follow the author's own exposition of his theology in his *Mirror of Charity*, joining to it the more original points of his theology in *Spiritual Friendship*, since these two treatises

1. *Spec.* I, 22, 525b.

are closely connected, in Aelred's mind, in the general perspective of Christian doctrine.

Love in Man

From the first page of his *Mirror of Charity*, which is his most remarkable and original work, Aelred shows how a very special gift of God confers a unique dignity on the rational creature and determines his destiny. This gift is love which orientates the soul towards God: "It comes of your own gift that it should love you."[2] By means of images and figures Aelred endeavors to describe the effects and define the nature of love: "What, O my God, is love? It is, if I mistake not, that spiritual, astonishing delight, so pleasant because so pure, its very gentleness the measure of its genuineness, bestowing gladness proportionate to its greatness. It is the heart's palate that tastes you, so pleasant; the eye that glimpses you, who are so kind and gracious; the place that enfolds you, the Infinite."[3]

In order to grasp the profound meaning and coherence of Aelred's teaching on charity and friendship we must start with the question: what is love in man? The discovery in man, who is God's image, of that "innate dynamism,"[4] at once a gift of God and an inclination towards him, is the first step in a spirituality and formation that has as its aim to guide the soul to the spiritual union of divine friendship. Aelred clearly explained the method he adopted in his study of charity: "I must investigate thoroughly the nature of this charity. Now, it is obvious that charity is love. . . . Hence deeper scrutiny is needful to make plain, first of all, what love means."[5] Years later he acknowledged that he had brought all his mental acumen to bear on the task of this analysis of love: "In my *Mirror* . . . I set out, as clearly and carefully as I could, the feelings and deeds that love gives rise to."[6]

2. *Spec.* I, 1, 506a.   3. *Spec.* I, 1, 505b.
4. *Spec.* I, 22, 525b: *vis quaedam naturalis.*
5. *Spec.* III, 7, 583d–584a.   6. *Am.*, 663b.

By his interest in the doctrine of love, Aelred of Rievaulx reveals himself in his truest form, reveals himself, too, as a child of his age. "Never, it can be said, did so many talk so much or so well of love as in this twelfth century. Never was love examined with such enthusiasm or fathomed with such penetrating keenness . . . , (it was) a vast warehouse that offered material to all the masters of the day."[7] The verve with which Aelred applied himself to the task was heightened by the fact that he seemed to be naturally predisposed to view all things, human and divine, through the eyes of love. Aelred's personality has to be taken into consideration in any exposition of his teaching, and this is especially true of his teaching on charity. Indeed, the most attractive and not the least profound feature of this great Abbot's teaching is the way in which he reveals himself in his writings. That teaching was certainly meant to be traditional, but it is nonetheless original, because it came from a man so attractive and affectionate, so full of life. We get the impression that this monk is teaching what he himself has practiced; his teaching was in tune with his inner life: there was no discordance between the ideal of the spiritual life explained in his works and his own way of living. His was an affective nature, like St Augustine's, that knew how to give itself and relished in an intense degree the joy of loving and being loved;[8] so he was naturally inclined to approach the mystery of God from the standpoint of love. Gifted with mental perspicacity, he had the good teacher's knack of observing others and took a delight in describing their inner actions and reactions.[9] Influenced by St Bernard's example and writings, and in any case requested by him with an urgency that left no room for refusal,[10] he wrote the *Mirror of Charity*, a masterpiece in its own way,[11] which is moreover to some extent the mirror of his own

7. G. Dumeige, *Richard de Saint-Victor et l'idée chrétienne de l'amour*, Paris, 1952, pp. 3 and 6.

8. *Am.*, Prologue, 659a.   9. *Spec.* III, 19, 592d.

10. *Epistola Bernardi Clarevallensis ad Aelredum*, P. L. 195, 501–502.

11. A. Wilmart, "L'instigateur du Speculum Caritatis d'Aelred, abbé de Rievaulx" in *Rev. Asc. Myst.* 14 (1935) 394.

soul. "Blessed Aelred of Rievaulx is the Doctor of spiritual love. He himself loved with an intense love. Even yet there is a warmth of feeling running through his works."[12]

While reflecting the prevailing thought of his day and his own personal feelings, Aelred's teaching on charity assumes its full significance only when set in its context—the history of salvation. Fr Bouyer has aptly remarked: "The central problem was presented as that of love, in its correlation with the restoration in us of the divine image, at present obscured by sin."[13] Those who have previously studied Aelred's teaching on charity clearly understand that this is the axis on which his whole doctrine turns.[14] As we have already noted, this divine gift of love inclines the image in the direction of its true destiny. Love's primary characteristic is, according to Aelred, to be "an intellect-endowed soul's power or property whereby it has the innate capacity of loving or not loving something."[15] This power is, in reality, identified with the will,[16] which explains why Aelred can speak indiscriminately of the intellect and love constituting free will,[17] or the reason and the will forming its components.[18] Love, the bent that is part of its being,[19]

---

12. A. Le Bail, "Aelred" in *Dict. Spir.* 1 (1937) col. 234.

13. L. Bouyer, *The Cistercian Heritage*, p. 134.

14. B. Pedrick, *Sancti Aelredi de caritate doctrina, Excerpta* . . . , pp. 5 and 6. Having shown that God is the source of charity, and described the divine image in the human soul, the author takes as the center of his thesis the history of the *Recessus* and *Reditus*: Ch. VI: *Pecatum Adae. Amissio similitudinis amore perverso.* Ch. VII: *Restauratio similitudinis rectificatione amoris.* P. Lucien van Boxsom is still more explicit: "The plan will adopt as far as possible the structure of the concrete object, as Aelred saw it, namely, the drama of man's destiny. Created for God, man turned away from his divine object, yet he preserves a basic rectitude which will permit him, with the aid of grace, to return to charity and God" (Dissertatio ad licentiam, *La doctrine de la charité de Saint Aelred*).

15. *Spec.* III, 7, 584a.

16. See Pedrick, *Sancti Ailredi de caritate doctrina, Excerpta* . . . , p. 18. S. Thomas, *In divin. Nomin.* IV, 19. P. Rousselot, *Pour l'histoire du problème de l'amour au Moyen Age*, p. 7, n. 2.

17. *Spec.* III, 8, 584c-d.   18. *Anima*, p. 108.   19. *Spec.* I, 22, 525b.

inclining every being towards its good and impelling it to its progressive perfection in the pursuit of its own end, is fundamentally the will.

By reason of this innate tendency called love, all creatures bear within them a reflection of God who is love. But while irrational beings can have only a trace of love, the human soul alone, excepting pure spirits, is favored with the truth of love, since a spirit is capable of intellectual love analogous to divine love.[20] Such a love, the privilege of the intelligent creature, is inseparably connected with the idea of image. As the image is a constitutive property of the soul as God created it, so love, an essential property of the image, is bestowed on man in the very act of creation: it belongs to man's nature to love. Even more, it is love, the love of the soul,[21] that reveals to it its true orientation and gives it its innate impulse or movement towards its Exemplar: since it came from God, it has a tendency to return to him.

This love-tendency is one of the primary meanings of the word *affectus* which has a range of meanings so rich and at the same time so indefinite that a translation of it would only impoverish or distort it. The concept of *affectus*[22] can cover the whole field of varied manifestations of the affective nature and is equally capable of expressing the highest acts of the will. These *affectus* were a favorite subject of Aelred's psychological study and, as we shall see in Part 3, one of the most interesting features of his theological speculation. In his *Mirror of Charity* he set himself to examine man's various *affectus* and his analysis is amazingly sharp and penetrating even today.[23] Love is one, and indeed the first, of these *affectus*, that is, a "spontaneous and pleasant attraction for someone,"[24] which definition needs to be amplified by the following description: "a

20. *Epistola ad Gilbertum*, P. L. 195, 361–362.
21. *Spec.* I, 1, 505b.
22. *Affectus*, one of the key words of medieval spirituality. Cf. J. Chatillon, "Cordis affectus" in *Dict. Spir.* II, col. 2288–2300.
23. J. Chatillon, *art. cit.,* col. 2294.   24. *Spec.* III, 9, 587d.

reason-accompanied affection whereby something is longingly sought and desired for its own sake, and on attainment is intimately and gratefully enjoyed, is cherished and kept safe."[25]

Before proceeding to examine the operations of the act of love, it is first of all necessary to underline the three characteristic qualities of the love-*affectus*: it is natural, spiritual and good. This notion of love is a guiding principle of Aelred's in his formative work of leading men back to God. The godward tendency is to be read in our divinely stamped nature. Undoubtedly there is need for another transcendent gift if man is to achieve the supernatural end God has been pleased to appoint him, but in this view of things even charity is seen as the right use, under the influence of grace, of the natural love proper to God's image. And since this end is union with God, the *affectus* tending to it cannot but be spiritual: spiritual union will be achieved by spiritual affection.[26] Love, as the fundamental inclination towards beatitude, is and always will be something good: this is undoubtedly one of the reasons for Aelred's humanism, which is one of the delightful aspects of his personality and doctrine. He believes in man and it is this principle of rectitude on which he builds his hope of renovation.

Love in man cannot be a blind impulse. Aelred proceeds to examine closely the three operations of love: election, application to act, and fruition.[27] Election is the choice made by the will, under the guidance of the reason, of an object for the purpose of enjoying it. This is a reasoned, not an instinctive choice: "reason ever goes with loving, not in the sense that love is always according to reason, but because loving ever means a clearly conscious preference for what is chosen over what is rejected."[28]

Under the term *application to act* Aelred includes everything that helps to achieve the possession and enjoyment of the object determined by the election; the choice of the object in fact "is closely

---

25. *Am.*, 663b.
27. *Spec.* III, 8, 584c.

26. *Spec.* I, 3, 507d.
28. *Ibid.*, 584d.

followed or rather accompanied by a scarcely perceptible *tending*
(*motus*) of love, that stirs and, to some extent, urges the soul to
desire what it has decided to choose."[29] The *motus*, therefore, includes both the internal stirring which is desire and the external
application which is act: "The soul is moved to desire when,
internally, it tends towards what it has judged worthy of enjoyment; it turns to action when some hidden dynamism of love
demands the doing of something externally."[30] Fruition consists in
using some good with pleasure and joy.[31] Therein love possesses
what it sought and rests in this enjoyment; it is the end attained by
the tendency of the soul that chose its object in order to enjoy it,
directed itself towards it and takes delight in it. So, concludes
Aelred, "charity or covetousness (that is, the use or abuse of love)
seems to consist in these three things . . . choice, the beginning of all
love, good or bad; tendency, its progress; enjoyment, its end."[32] It
should be noted, however, that there is no love without enjoyment;[33] love is formally defined by fruition; everything is directed
to that. Undoubtedly to enjoy some object presupposes that the
memory and reason already possess it. In a rational being the three
faculties of the soul cooperate in the achievement of beatitude,[34]
but fruition is identified with perfect possession: "memory provides
in plenty, intellect penetrates to the depths; but what delight comes
of it should attention to both thoughts and findings be lacking
the will?"[35]

Not every enjoyment, however, is true happiness; there is only
one beatitude befitting the soul that is God's image and this is the
possession of the Supreme Good. Whatever other object a disordered love may will and enjoy, it cannot bestow on the soul the
peace that brings bliss; it may give some passing pleasure but it
ultimately breeds misery, the lot of the soul that turns away from

29. *Ibid.*, 585a.   30. *Spec.* III, 10, 587b.   31. *Spec.* III, 8, 585a.
32. *Ibid.*, 585b.   33. *Spec.* I, 4, 508b.   34. *Spec.* I, 4, 508a.
35. *Ibid.*, 508b.

the true Good: "to delight in utter baseness is extreme wretchedness."[36] The beatitude of any being lies in the possession of its end.
Now man's end is God;[37] according to God's plan, man is destined
to share in his divine life; his nature, as actually constituted by God,
is ordained to this end, and no other is capable of bringing him true
beatitude. The longing for beatitude,[38] which is another name for
love, is so rooted in our very being that the human soul will never
find rest until it has reached "what is highest, best, second to none,
all-surpassing."[39] It will never be satisfied as long as it is not filled
by God; he alone is "the beatitude of all the blessed."[40]

But this ultimate participation in God's beatitude supposes a
common element to start with, some initial participation in the
form of a rudimentary likeness: the ordination to the end should be
revealed in man's very nature. If "intellectual creatures alone are
capable of such beatitude that is because, made in the image of their
Creator, they are able to cling to him whose images they are."[41]
This union is achieved by the three faculties constituting the soul;
all three cooperate in achieving beatitude, but union is strictly love's
achievement. The whole question of beatitude, therefore, is reduced
to an assimilation, in the etymological sense of the word, which will
be the work of love.

Thus even from the moment of its constitution, human nature
has been appointed the goal it must tend to. It has within it a law
that points it towards this goal, an inclination urging it towards its
destiny, a gravitation drawing it towards its center, the center of its
rest, which is God. This attraction henceforth will not quit man no
matter where he may choose to wander. If the image rejects God,
he will never arrive at that blissful "Sabbath," the complete rest in
the possession of the fully satisfying good.

In such a view, love is really at the heart of the problem of man.
Love it is that makes him capable of union with God, love "assimi-

36. *Ibid.,* 508a.   37. *Spec.* I, 3, 508a.   38. *Spec.* I, 22, 526a.
39. *Ibid.,* 525b.   40. *Spec.* I, 3, 507d.   41. *Ibid.*

lates" him to God, and, under the direction of charity, will restore the image to the likeness of God. Very truly, then, can Aelred conclude with this lapidary sentence:

> "Keep charity and nothing will be wanting to you;
> lose it and nothing . . . will profit you."[42]

God is Friendship

We approach the mystery of God, then, by first considering created love. The study of love in man leads to the contemplation of love in God. The soul is God's image, is marked by and has need of him, chiefly by reason of its love. Love tends to God because it is a gift that comes from him and wants to return to its source. The capacity created in it is a call to union with God, according to the law of return to God: "like seeks its like"; "To love you is to hold you close in proportion to the love; you are love, charity."[43]

The general notion of love as a longing for beatitude, a natural desire for the beatitude proper to the rational soul, is seen by Aelred to fit into the overall picture of the cosmos and the laws governing it: all beings seek their center of equilibrium, the state of rest corresponding to their nature and coinciding with the possession of the end appointed by their Creator. Every being tends towards its own particular position, seeks its proper place. Away from this place, it is restless; rest is to be found only there.[44] Aelred borrows examples, those of a stone and oil for instance, from St Augustine,[45] to illustrate this universal law: "Throw a stone up into the air. Soon, as though against its will, does not its weight force it down? . . . Pour some other fluid into oil. Impatient of such treatment, the oil begins to work its way to the surface, gives itself no rest until,

42. *Spec.* I, 16, 520b.   43. *Spec.* I, 1, 505c.
44. *Spec.* I, 21, 524c.   45. *Conf.* XIII, 9, 10.

E

surpassing the other element, it finds the tranquillity of its rightful place."[46] The same tendency is equally manifest in vegetables as in animals: when they have obtained their satisfaction, "with naught else to desire, they take their rest."[47] Man is no exception to this rule. With unabated energy, he too tends towards his fulfillment and peace in the enjoyment of his end. But where does this rest for a human being lie? Made in God's image, become capable of receiving him by love, he finds his rest only in loving him: "Who love you, find their rest in you; true rest, tranquillity, peace, the soul's very Sabbath."[48]

So the examination of the deep-reaching nature of man and the essential tendencies of his soul lead us to study the mystery of God. Here, it seems, we reach the apex of Aelred's theology and the heart of his treatise on charity, "one of the rare metaphysical *dicta* in his work. We must recognize its grandeur"[49] and the source of his inspiration, which is revelation. According to Fr Aelred Squire OP,[50] St Aelred reveals in chapters 19–21 of Book I theological insight of rare depth which gives a unique coherence to his speculation on man and God.

It was his reading of the Scriptures, his pondering on the first chapters of Genesis, that led Aelred to this view of God. He contemplates him first in his creative activity. What grandeur in each of those six days, when wonderful things sprang forth from the hands of God![51] But the contemplative Aelred, while admiring the way in which God accomplishes this creation, wants to know the reason for it. Not because of any need or necessity did the Creator bring all these creatures into being: "You had fancied him in your image, a creator who lacked pleasant sight, restful enjoyment . . . whereas he wants for nothing, being all-sufficient, in every way, to himself."[52] In a mysterious way this divine plenitude is suggested

46. *Spec.* I, 21, 524c.   47. *Ibid.*, 525a.   48. *Spec.* I, 18, 521b.
49. L. Bouyer, *The Cistercian Heritage*, p. 135.
50. In a study as yet unpublished.   51. *Spec.* I, 19, 521d–522a.
52. *Ibid.*, 522c.

by the seventh day, which rivets Aelred's attention and stirs him to wonder: "Great day this, great this rest, the great Sabbath! Let not its meaning escape you." While the first six days presented God's work in progressive stages—Scripture here accommodates itself to our way of conceiving an activity unfolding itself in time—the seventh day, on the contrary, appears of a different order. The succession of six days, each with its morning and evening, symbolizes the "instability of every created thing, its growth and decay, beginning and ending," but the seventh day has "neither morning nor evening," it is outside the sphere of the created, it belongs to the realm of the divine: "God's day of rest is outside time, eternal."[53] The seventh day is the key to the divine mystery; it is the reason for God's creative activity, the end of all creation, because it is God's Sabbath.

This rest, the supreme activity, is charity: "God's rest, as before stated, is his love."[54] And there, pin-pointed for us, is that insight of Aelred's which, so simply yet so profoundly, links up the first pages of Genesis with the final message of revelation from the lips of St John—"God is love"—by leading to its sublime fulfillment all the yearning for peace and rest and sabbath that runs through the Bible from beginning to end.[55] And at the topmost point of creation, there appears transcendent the mysterious Rest that is God's very being: "That God should ever rest in his blissful love, most tranquil will, more than abounding kindness, is another way of saying that he is."[56] In his Sabbath which is love, God *is* and brings all things into being: "His only reason for creating . . . (was) to give scope to his love's bounty . . . bold in its sweep from world's end to world's end, everywhere manifesting its gracious ordering, both exemplar and cause of peace."[57]

Already in chapter 5 of the *Mirror of Charity*, when he spoke of

---

53. *Ibid.*, 522b.   54. *Spec.* I, 20, 523c.
55. A yearning that is expressed by the biblical terms *peace, rest, Sabbath, dwelling*, etc.
56. *Spec.* I, 19, 523a.   57. *Ibid.*, 522c–d.

the restoration of the image in us, Aelred had given the soul, toiling on the return path, a glimpse of the vision of peace and unity of the Trinity, source and exemplar of all beatitude: "Peace, quiet, happiness such as this awaits us in the homeland of our hope. . . . Eternal, unfailing love, eternity true and desirable, everlasting, final and ravishing Trinity! Yes, rest for us is there, and peace; blessed quiet and quiet blessedness, true and sure joy. . . . All this is there and perfectly and only there."[58]

This view of God as love is the theological apex of Aelred's *Mirror of Charity*, yet it certainly does not exhaust all his speculation on the meaning of man and his divine destiny. The human soul is called indeed to be like God, but a God who is love and triune, whose life is a communion of Persons in the transcendent unity of one and the same nature: "What loving exchange this, joyful embrace, the blissful love wherein Father and Son abide in one another!"[59] Living and indescribable friendship! Aelred elaborates this point in his treatise *On Spiritual Friendship*. When his friend and disciple, Yvo, ventures to render the text of St John as "God is friendship," Aelred raises no objection; indeed he has no hesitation in following up with the other half of the verse as "He who dwells in friendship dwells in God and God in him."[60] If, therefore, we are not to restrict or distort Aelred's doctrine on charity we must not neglect to examine his theology of spiritual friendship, which he called "a most sacred kind of love."[61]

His doctrine on spiritual friendship fits into his whole theology with a simplicity and breadth of view that is important to underline. While, on the one hand, this inclination to friendship is something innate in man, it corresponds at the same time to God's inscrutable plan by which he willed this spiritual exchange between rational creatures after the example of the uninterrupted and mysterious exchange within the Trinity. God has launched no creature into

58. *Spec.* I, 5, 509b–c.
60. *Am.,* 670a; ed. Dubois, p. 45.

59. *Spec.* I, 20, 523c.
61. *Spec.* III, 39, 619b.

isolated existence: "His will and decree are that all creatures should abide in tranquillity and community, thus sharing, to some extent, and suggesting, the unity of the Unique and Absolute."[62] Furthermore the flowering of friendship in our life makes us more fully men, since true friendship springs from "the high estate of man and his heart's longing;"[63] while the lack of it in a human being is a sign of the degradation that makes him like the brute beast: "They are no better than the beasts, who give the name of life to living without friendship, without loving and being loved."[64] If you shut out friendship, you shut out the sunlight of human life,[65] and you no longer will your own good. This latter statement is no exaggeration but a faithful interpretation of the mind of Aelred, for whom love of self is the model of friendship. My friend is another self whom I must love as myself. Here Aelred parts company with Cicero, who reduced friendship to an altruistic inclination, and is at one with St Thomas, who was later to teach as had the Abbot of Rievaulx.[66]

There is a remarkable passage in the sermon for Pentecost[67] which throws light on the whole question of friendship and links it with the theology of the Trinity. First of all Aelred recalls the idea of the infinite happiness of God who has no need of creatures in order to be happy, a train of thought which is found in *On Spiritual Friendship* also: "God, supreme in power, in goodness, is his own sufficiency, his own goodness, joy, glory, beatitude. . . . More, he is the sufficiency of all else . . . universal fount of existence, life and understanding."[68]

But God in his happiness willed to create beings in the image of

---

62. *Am.*, 667a; ed. Dubois, p. 34.

63. *Am.*, 666b; p. 30.   64. *Am.*, 676c; p. 80.

65. *Am.*, 676b; pp. 76–78. This is a quotation from Cicero: *Solem, inquit, e mundo tollere videntur, qui amicitiam e vita tollunt* . . . : "He seems, he says, to shut out the sun from the world, who shuts friendship out of his life . . ."

66. Cf. G. Vansteenberghe, "Amitié" in *Dict. Spir.*, t. I (1937) col. 506.

67. *S. Ined.*, p. 108.   68. *Am.*, 666d–667a, pp. 32–34.

his trinitarian happiness, promoting their own happiness by doing good to one another. He thus bestowed on them the gift of helpfulness. At the end of this first part, we shall see the importance of this idea in the whole of Aelred's doctrine. Thus "many rational creatures were made, yet made of one same nature, that even to outward seeming their interchange of good offices might be a multiple reflection of the goodwill of God."[69]

God, who is friendship and whose life is an unending interchange so perfect that we cannot even imagine it, willed that friendship should exist between his creatures, so that they might be true images of himself. Friendship has love for its principle[70] and is, besides, its perfection, because love tends towards union, even to a kind of unity: "Love, caring only for unity of nature, so unites things of one nature that they become one heart and one soul."[71]

Aelred lays great stress on this unifying power of love. Spiritual friendship, as he conceived it, is not easy and could never be common, for it demands "oneness of will."[72] Accordingly how should charity not be friendship, and that in an eminent way, since it is "the closest union of God's will and man's"?[73] Aelred goes a step further and sees the very problem of man as a question of friendship. The harmony of the human will with the divine is the remedy for the discord caused by sin: spiritual friendship is the way to God.

In the first place, true friendship, "agreement in what pertains to God and man," can exist only between those who are good,[74] those who have accepted the yoke of the Lord[75] and belong to Christ. Here again Christ appears as the indispensable Mediator, the meeting ground of true friendship; this is a point on which Aelred is most explicit: "My conviction is that outside Christ true friendship is impossible."[76] Spiritual friendship "begins in Christ, perseveres

69. S. Ined., p. 108.

71. Epistola ad Gilbertum, P.L. 195, 361–362.

73. Spec. II, 18, 566c.   74. Am., 666c; p. 31.

76. Am., 663a.

70. Am., 686c; p. 128.

72. Am., 673d; p. 66.

75. Spec. I, 27, 531a.

only if Christ is its norm, and looks to Christ for its perfection and efficacy. Its birth, the course of its development, its full achievement is Christ."⁷⁷

We shall not appreciate the penetrating originality of Aelred's theology if we do not pause to study his concept of friendship in relation to God. The preceding chapter gave an account of the history of the human soul that has to return to God by way of Christ; here spiritual friendship is presented as a union with Christ and a way leading to God: "Friendship is like a step to raise us to the love and knowledge of God." Aelred makes an even greater claim: "friendship lies close to perfection."⁷⁸ If the friendship that unites two friends is true, that is to say spiritual, Christ becomes more and more their common center of attraction and union: "Friend of man becomes friend of God;"⁷⁹ "Suppose you are praying on your friend's behalf to Christ . . . so easy and inevitable is it for your affection to pass from one to the other that, in no time, Christ himself has become the object of your love and desire."⁸⁰ If Aelred did not develop the trinitarian concept of friendship, which was a favorite theme of Richard of Saint-Victor, he does, however, allude to it, which shows that the idea was not unknown to him: "Here we are, you and I; and Christ, I hope, is the third who unites us."⁸¹ Christ is present in every true spiritual friendship and, in his union with the Father, is the model of the intimacy that should exist between friends;⁸² yet more, he is the perfection of friendship: a friend "goes forward with his friend to Christ's friendship and to becoming one spirit with him."⁸³

But here, too, Christ must play the role of redeemer and restorer. By breaking off his friendship with God, man at the same time perverted his inclination to union with his fellowmen. Our first parents, because they were made by God in his image and likeness,

77. *Am.*, 662b–c; pp. 10–12.   78. *Am.*, 672a; p. 56.
79. *Am.*, 671d; p. 56.   80. *Am.*, 701b; p. 201.   81. *Am.*, 661a; p. 6.
82. *Am.*, 691c; p. 154.   83. *Am.*, 672d; p. 60.

loved each other with mind and heart,[84] with a charity that was pure and delightful friendship.[85] They lived in harmony with each other and with everything else, both divine and human: conformity is a property of friendship.[86] By cupidity, that is, perverse love of self, man preferred his own private good to the common good and hence "quarrels, jealousies, spite and suspicion go to make men's depraved doings."[87] The lovely flower of spiritual friendship no longer grows naturally in these warped souls, souls coiled back on themselves, because "it is impossible for honest men and rogues to achieve conformity of will and purpose."[88] Man's love, then, needs to undergo a process of restoration if it is to become charity anew and this charity flower into friendship. The journeying of man on earth will be marked by a long, persistent struggle between the selfishness that closes him in on himself and the friendship which will restore harmony between himself, his fellowmen and God. The full realization of this opening-out process of the human person in community with others will be achieved only in heaven. In the concluding pages of *On Spiritual Friendship* we are given a glimpse of man's happiness and God's triumph, when our charity will be nothing but all-embracing friendship: "Spiritual friendship, confined to so few at present, will overflow then to all our neighbors and thence to God, to God who will be all in all" (1 Cor 15:28).[89]

Cupidity or Friendship

"Man, when he was in honor, did not understand." How strange a deviation! In his nature as in his activity, man was orientated towards God; he knew that in God his happiness was to be found and yet he sought it elsewhere. How was such a turning away possible? For Aelred the basic explanation of this deviation is a

84. *Spec.* III, 20, 594c.   85. *Am.*, 667d; p. 36.   86. *Am.*, 662c; p. 12.
87. *Am.*, 668a; p. 38.   88. *Ibid.*   89. *Am.*, 702b; p. 200.

question of love: withdrawal from God was the consequence of love's deliberate choice.[90] In this sentence we get a very interesting hint of the way Aelred thinks of sin, the turning away from God. If we would understand the "mystery of iniquity" we must start with an analysis of the notion of love. Sin is a perversion of love. Man estranges himself from God because he loves some created good more than the Supreme Good. In this, man is seeking his happiness, but not the beatitude which alone befits his status as an image of God.

To understand how such a perversion could come about, we have to realize that fruition can be considered from two points of view; we can consider the subject and the object of fruition. The subject finds in the possession of the object a personal satisfaction, delight, rest, fulfillment of its desire and it enjoys such a state.[91] But there is a relationship and donation of the subject to the object; the subject tends to unite itself with it, to pass into it, to give itself to it and to lose itself in it: "To love you is to hold you close in proportion to the love. . . . You are the rich fountain of which your friends drink deep, and, lost in you, forget themselves."[92] The Sabbath of charity consists in the subject's possession of the object and the object's possession of the subject: "that God possesses him and he possesses God; that he belongs to God and God to him; that he is God's captive and God is his."[93] In a letter to a friend, Aelred describes the two aspects of this delight of love: "Swept away by affection, my intention stops not at anything of yours . . . plunges deep into your very self to share your feelings and thoughts, your very soul. . . . There I see how good you are, hold and share your wisdom, experience your charm and am made glad."[94]

In the last analysis the essential element in love is its relation to the object loved. Our love is not turned back on our own enjoyment as such, but is totally directed to the object loved, not con-

90. *Spec.* I, 7, 512a; I, 8, 512b.   91. *S. Temp.* XVIII, 316a.
92. *Spec.* I, 1, 505c.   93. *Spec.* III, 6, 583a.
94. *Epistola ad Gilbertum,* P.L. 195, 361–362.

sidered as something external to ourselves, but as possessed by us, and more especially, as possessing us by way of union with itself. Our love goes astray precisely when we seek our own enjoyment as object. When a man seeks fruition in its subjective aspect, he stops short at himself instead of uniting himself with the sovereign Good. Man should have tended, following the natural inclination of his intellect-endowed soul, towards "what is highest,"[95] but he "deflected" his love to a less worthy object.[96] This was to rebel, to play the wanton, to turn back on himself, and this left him ensnared and "blinded by his own cupidity,"[97] all coiled back on himself.[98]

Aelred dwells at length on this perverted love, which is what cupidity is, and often describes the havoc it plays in the heart of a monk.[99] It is easy to understand this insistence of his, because, if God is the end of all creatures and love is the force that draws them to him, then there can be no more fatal deviation, no more radical disorder, than that of a love which, in turning away from God, coils back on itself. If charity is the be-all of God and of man, cupidity is the root of all evils.[100]

The study of the concept of cupidity in Aelred's doctrine leaves us with the impression—an impression we get more than once in reading through his works—that the Abbot of Rievaulx, while not so complex or profound as St Bernard, has the gift of clarity, which at times perhaps is an obstacle to depth of thought. For Aelred cupidity is the contrary of charity; the two are completely incompatible; while Bernard, on the other hand, can write: "Charity will never lack cupidity."[101] Similarly Richard of Saint-Victor does not think that charity is necessarily opposed to cupidity.[102] According

---

95. *Spec.* I, 22, 525a.   96. *Spec.* I, 4, 508b.   97. *Ibid.,* 508c.

98. *S. Ined.,* p. 123; Charity will rectify the soul: *Ubi nichil iniquum, nichil curvum, distortum nichil . . .*

99. *Spec.* I, 7–40: II, 2–4 and 21–26.

100. 1 Tim 6:10. Cf. *Spec.* III, 8, 585c.

101. *De diligendo Deo,* P.L. 182, 998a.

102. See G. Dumeige, *Richard de Saint-Victor et l'idée chrétienne de l'amour,* p. 60, n. 4.

to these two writers, cupidity, taken in its generic sense, can embrace the ideas of willing, affection and love, and should gradually undergo a process of purification and be progressively set in order as it passes through the various degrees of love. But for Aelred any rectification of cupidity is inconceivable; cupidity cannot be set in order, since it is essentially evil of its very nature. As he sees it, it must be destroyed, not purified.[103]

Between cupidity and charity, therefore, there exists a very clear-cut distinction, which Aelred, we find, is careful to preserve throughout his doctrine. Man's lot is decided between these two opposing forces. Those who follow the downward trend are separated from God, "since they have preferred the detours of cupidity to the direct route of charity."[104] Those who are motivated by charity become more and more like to God.

Whether the natural power of loving becomes cupidity or charity depends upon the consent of the free will,[105] although his unaided human strength is not sufficient to restore a man to charity and make him increase in it.[106] The whole spiritual life, therefore, will bear the mark of a conflict in which human liberty, cooperating with divine grace, gradually substitutes charity for cupidity and restores the image bit by bit, but this means effort, ascesis, the toil involved in the return of the prodigal son.[107]

The human soul, lost in the land of unlikeness, remains God's image. So the power of loving, which is connatural to it, is still alive in it and, as a vital power, continues to seek its good in order to enjoy it. It is on this continuance of love in the soul of the sinner, tormented by the desire for beatitude, that Aelred bases his hope of renewal, with, to be sure, the help of God, who is ever ready to intervene in order to accomplish his own work,[108] which is mercy.

103. See B. Pedrick, *Sancti Ailredi* . . . , *Excerpta,* p. 50.
104. *Spec.* I, 15, 519c.   105. *Spec.* I, 9 and 10; 513d.
106. *Spec.* I, 10, 513d.   107. *S. Temp.* XXI, 334c–d.
108. *S. Temp.* XII, 280d.

Moreover, Aelred encourages man to seek his happiness with more and more earnestness, for, by way of this very quest, he will come to realize the futility of the transient goods that are incapable of fulfilling his desire: "Wonderful creature of God, only less than God, why this folly? How can you love a world so unworthy of you? . . . Go on with your seeking, but not as hitherto. Seek rather for what alone will quiet your longing and bring you rest. Yes, seek that."[109] The purpose of such exhortations is to teach the soul that God alone is true beatitude and that the possession of him by charity is man's true Sabbath.[110]

But before it reaches this blissful rest, the soul has a long road to travel in its quest of God, and a painful toil of restoration to submit to.[111] It means in fact that it has to set about the task of reorientating its love in the right direction by gradually removing the evil leaven of cupidity.[112] Charity achieves the initial change or spiritual circumcision,[113] which is Christian conversion; charity too brings about the progressive transition of the soul from being carnal to being spiritual; and finally it is likewise charity that tends to open the soul to true friendship by coordinating the three loves.

The soul that starts off completely bent in on itself by disordered love is straightened up, is converted and directs anew its natural power of love towards God.[114] By agreeing thus with its divine Exemplar, the image renews the lost likeness in itself; love becomes charity once more. But before the soul, reformed in this way,[115] is a marvel of ordered beauty[116] through the perfect restoration of the image, divine charity and man's cupidity have to come to grips in a painful and persistent struggle. Charity, like "oil of the spirit,"[117] will only slowly heal the wounds of the soul and expel the "dregs of the old self."[118] During his earthly wayfaring, man will be the

109. *Spec.* I, 23, 526b-c.
110. *Spec.* I, 18, 521b.
111. *S. Temp.* XXI, 328a.
112. *S. Temp.* XII, 278d.
113. *S. Oner.* XXIX, 489d.
114. *Spec.* I, 8, 512b.
115. *S. Ined.*, p. 34.
116. *S. Ined.*, p. 123.
117. *S. Temp.* XII, 278c.
118. *Spec.* I, 9, 513b.

battlefield and at the same time the prize at stake in this struggle between charity, that would raise him to God, and cupidity, that presses heavily on him to drag him back to the land of unlikeness: "Charity lifts up the soul to the purpose of its creation; cupidity bows it to slavery of its own choosing."[119]

On this point Aelred leaves us in no doubt: there can be no escaping this spiritual struggle.[120] If we do not accept it, we reject the Christian way of returning to God. "To shirk spiritual warfare means refusing to be a man."[121] The man who thinks he can share in Christ's resurrection without sharing in his passion is deluding himself.[122] Christians are, by their profession, "heralds of the Cross of Christ."[123] The necessity for asceticism is derived from the specific character of our going to God, which takes the form of a return, a reparation, a restoration. Abnegation becomes a vital necessity for anyone who has preferred other goods, the enjoyment of which is incompatible with the possession of the true Good. There is need for a new life to be initiated by way of a spiritual circumcision,[124] for purification,[125] for bonds to be broken,[126] if the soul is not to remain captive like a bird that cannot fly.[127] Over and over again Aelred states or intimates that without asceticism there can be no mysticism. If we would reach the heights,[128] we must pay the price. This is the reason why some souls are raised to the heights—they have allowed themselves to be thoroughly purified. But the lukewarm, when faced with the toil, run away: "Who draw back at the first hint of difficulty . . . have closed the door to the delights I speak of, and, for all their trouble, will never enjoy the high comfort of such experience."[129]

This asceticism should not be regarded merely in its negative

119. *Spec.* I, 8, 513a.   120. *S. Temp.* XXI, 334d.
121. *S. Temp.* XV, 294d.   122. *S. Temp.* XII, 282d.
123. *Spec.* II, 1, 547b.   124. *S. Oner.* XXIX, 489d, also *S. Ined.*, p. 103.
125. *S. Temp.* IV, 237c.   126. *S. Temp.* XXI, 331b.
127. *S. Oner.* XXVIII, 482d.
128. *S. Ined.*, p. 103.   129. *Spec.* II, 13, 557c-d.

aspect of abnegation and mortification. Indeed it has ultimately no meaning save as a means to man's fulfillment. Sin had disrupted his internal unity and harmony with his fellow creatures and God, and so had alienated him. The work of renewal restores him to himself, to his neighbors and to God.[130]

This teaches us what is in Aelred's eyes the chief enemy of our restoration, the one he most often refers to and the one that is most to be feared, because most artful and pernicious. It is self-will, a most inveterate species of cupidity, with all the opposition to the divine will and resistance to the divine action implied in this word "self" (*proprium*).[131] It is thoroughly bad since at every moment charity is in danger of being counteracted and its restorative action frustrated by it. It spoils the finest spiritual endeavors, forcing its subjects into a form of slavery from which it is exceedingly difficult to escape.[132] It is against this radical evil that the self-restraint (*abstinentia*) Aelred preached so much[133] must be directed. Since sin is the result of this self-will, irregularly turned in on itself, restoration will be the work of Christian love that is a participation of God: "This renewal can be achieved only by obeying the new commandment of charity. . . . Such obedience is the putting off of the old self, the soul's renovation and recovery of the divine likeness. Nothing keeps our wretched affection stuck fast in clinging sensuality (as though its own tendency towards baseness were not sufficiently strong) except cupidity; . . . once, however, heaven-sent charity has its way . . . it removes all such old habits and clothes us anew."[134]

As Aelred sees it, man's problem always comes down to the same choice between self-love, which makes him a sinner, and divine love, which sets him free. The rectifying of his love is attended with constant struggle, a fact that beginners soon learn by experience:

130. *S. Ined.*, p. 57.   131. *S. Ined.*, p. 128.   132. *S. Ined.*, pp. 56, 60.
133. Aelred insists a great deal on the *abstinentia, virtutum omnium nutrix* (*S. Ined.*, p. 64).
134. *Spec.* I, 8, 512c

"every newcomer to the spiritual life makes generous efforts in new-found charity, to reach the heights . . . but old cupidity keeps him back."[135] With successive ups and downs, victories and defeats, the battle will go on throughout the entire span of this earthly life, and it is only by degrees that peace of soul will be secured, as charity triumphs over the three concupiscences, the three fundamental forms of cupidity.[136]

It would be inadequate and incorrect to restrict the role of charity to combating cupidity and extirpating its poisoned roots. Much more important is its constructive and vital function of redirecting the soul's powers towards God with increasing depth and intensity. It has to permeate the activities of the soul, transforming them into virtues, virtue here being understood as a rectification that proceeds from God and draws things to him: "Virtue . . . and its reward, beatitude, constitute the land of likeness; vice and wretchedness, the land of unlikeness. . . . The more a man indulges vice, the less like God he becomes, and, consequently, the further he withdraws from God; while the greater his virtue, the greater his likeness, and, therefore, the greater his closeness to him."[137]

Viewed in this way, the role of charity in ordering and co-ordinating the virtues is clearly apparent. According to Aelred, there is no genuine virtue in a man without charity: "Faith is not effective as a virtue unless it expresses itself in love, nor hope which does not love its object. . . . What is temperance, except love unduped by pleasure? Prudence—what is it but love which error has not led astray? Fortitude—is it not love unyielding in adversity? Justice—fair-dealing love. . . ."[138]

Aelred arrives at this epigrammatic conclusion: "Love, then, finds its beginning in faith, its practice in the other virtues, but its perfection in itself."[139]

To bring out charity's primacy in the hierarchy of the virtues,

135. *Spec.* II, 21, 570a. 136. *Spec.* II, 21–26.
137. *S. Oner.* VII, 391c-d. 138. *Spec.* I, 31, 536a. 139. *Ibid.*

Aelred composed an allegorical heptameron, in which each virtue corresponds to one of the days of creation and derives some special significance from it. The divine work culminates in charity, the spiritual Sabbath: "All this achieved, there comes the rest that definitely ends our troubles; I mean charity, perfection of all the virtues, delightful refreshment of the holy, noblest rule of all behavior; it lies at the root of whatever perfection good deeds have."[140]

Charity, moreover, is the crown of the virtues; it alone is the fulfillment of their impulse towards God, for it alone, by way of intimate union with the Sovereign Good, procures true beatitude.[141]

Our Lord, unseen yet present, watches over the soul's ascent to God. At certain moments he makes his presence felt; he *visits* the soul with various graces for the purpose of helping it to achieve more effectively the rectification of its affections. Aelred examines these visitations of the Lord in several chapters of his *Mirror of Charity*[142] where he sets himself to explain what they are for, what they do, and what they produce. Although this treatise could easily be styled a treatise on compunction (understood in the broad sense as a spirit pervading the entire life of the soul on its journey to God), Aelred's real purpose is to describe three stages of the spiritual life. In a systematic series of tripartite divisions, a literary device much in vogue at that period, he endeavors to discover the action and growth of charity on this journey, where pain and joy succeed each other, and where man's efforts and God's grace coalesce.

The first visitation rouses the soul to genuine conversion and urges it to a better way of life. If the soul responds, it will be led forward; if it refuses, it will be held to account.[143] When the soul has shaken off its torpor and is willing to fight and endure weariness for the love of Christ, it receives encouragement to persevere by a second visit: "Encouragement amid grief; breathing-space for the

---

140. *Spec.* I, 32, 537b.
142. *Spec.* II, 7–16, 553–561.

141. *Spec.* I, 33, 538a–b.
143. *Spec.* II, 8–9, 554a–b.

weary; defense in temptation; food for the journey."[144] Finally at the third visitation the Lord crowns his gifts: his justice in unison with his mercy perfects every good in this rare and sublime visit, when the soul begins to experience some foretaste of its reward.[145]

Aelred summarizes the three visitations as follows: "The soul is awakened in the first stage, purified in the second, enjoys sabbath-rest in the third. In the first degree mercy has its way, in the second kindness, in the third justice. Mercy searches for the wanderer; once found, kindness reinstates him; when perfect, justice rewards him."[146] It is evident that he is dealing with three moments in the spiritual life marked by visits that bring help to the soul on its way to God.

In his treatise *On Spiritual Friendship*, Aelred, true to his humanistic outlook, draws on the language of friends for an image to describe the progressive spiritualizing of love that is becoming more and more true friendship, namely, the symbol of the three kisses: "Let us look into the meaning of a kiss on the mouth, and learn what is spiritual and divine from what is external and human. . . . In such a kiss two breaths meet, mingle and are made one. . . . We may speak, then, of a kiss that is external, of another that is spiritual, of a third that is mystical; external if lips meet, spiritual if minds join, mystical if God's Spirit and his gifts are at work." From which Aelred draws a very beautiful idea of friendship: "the kiss of Christ," who breathes this holy affection into those who really love each other, and who leads such friends to the kiss of mystical union.[147]

Only by opening himself by charity to friendship with God and with other men in this way does a man truly love himself, and after the toil, the just deserts of his cupidity, find rest in the possession of his good. Love's rest is called a Sabbath by Aelred, who in this is following a school of thought whose chief exponent seems to be

---

144. *Spec.* II, 10, 555a.   145. *Spec.* II, 556b.   146. *Spec.* II, 11, 555c.
147. *Am.*, 672d–673d, pp. 60–66.

F

St Maximus the Confessor:[148] "The spiritual Sabbath is rest to the soul, peace to the heart, quiet to the mind."[149] Now a human being, made for God, will find his true rest only in him. There exists for man no true Sabbath outside of God, and "its exclusive place and price is love":[150] "Who love you, find their rest in you."[151]

In the heavenly homeland alone will there be true and lasting rest, but even here on earth the man who loves God enjoys moments of peaceful calm which are a foretaste of the everlasting Sabbath: indeed love itself is even now an astonishing delight.[152] Furthermore, in the *Mirror of Charity* Aelred distinguishes and analyses these various successive but related fruitions which mark the soul's progress. This is a noteworthy aspect of his teaching,[153] which it is important to underline in order to understand the complexity of our loves in the unity of charity. Since as a matter of fact charity has three objects—oneself, one's neighbor and God—each of these three objects will have its particular Sabbath, not isolated from the other two, but closely and necessarily connected with them by reason of the unifying property of supernatural charity.

To give an accurate and balanced account of his ideas, Aelred at times emphasizes the organic unity of these three loves: " . . . so obviously a trinity, are a marvellous unity. Each of them is found in both the others and all are found in each; if one is present, all are; if one fails, all do."[154] At other times he describes the psychological features that distinguish them: "Though these three loves are inseparable, yet they are not equally experienced at all times. At one time the sense of rest and gladness comes of interior purity; at another time it proceeds from the pleasant concord of brotherly

---

148. See Urs von Balthasar, *Die gnostischen Centurien des Maximus Confessor (Coll. Freiburger theolog. Studien,* LXI. Heft, pp. 14, 115, 118 and 120).

149. *Spec.* III, 2, 577c.   150. *Spec.* II, 1, 546d.

151. *Spec.* I, 18, 521b.   152. *Spec.* I, 1, 505b.

153. A. Le Bail, *Les traités de la charité dans l'Ordre de Cîteaux,* t. I, p. 88.

154. *Spec.* III, 2, 577d.

affection; at yet another, it is caused, and all the more abundantly, by divine contemplation."[155]

Aelred's analysis brings out the distinguishing mark of each Sabbath by indicating the increasingly higher degree of coordination. Love of self is a necessity, "it forms part of our nature," but it requires effort to orientate it in the right direction. When "we have done our duty in the way of recollection, mortification and obedience, and interior purity has proved that we truly love ourselves . . . all is gladness, concord, peace, rest, . . . like a happy household about its parent."[156]

When the union of the soul, "cemented by love to the souls of all its brethren," advances to such an extent that it now becomes but one heart and one soul with them, and embraces the entire human race in a single act of spiritual love, then is celebrated the second Sabbath, when the soul knows by experience how good and pleasant a thing it is for brethren to dwell together.[157] Such a peace is not attained without tedious toil, to which Aelred alludes in his comparison with the six mystical years in preparation for this Sabbath.[158] The third Sabbath, that of divine love, has this special characteristic that it precedes, accompanies and at once perfects the other two, for "it is their very life," without which they would not even exist.[159] It is the love of God that moves us to the other loves.[160] There is no rightly directed love of self, in fact, which is not some initial love of God, and if we would love our neighbor truly, we must needs have a divine seed of love within our hearts.[161] And this seed, when it grows, finally comes to give life to all and perfects all. The coordination of the three loves is due to this fact: "Love for God makes such a wondrous progress that it draws those other two loves, mere tiny sparks, into its ever more fervent abundance and so concentrates the soul's whole affection . . . on God."[162] Then it is

155. *Spec.* III, 2, 578b–c.   156. *Spec.* III, 3, 579a and 578d.
157. *Spec.* III, 4, 581b.   158. *Spec.* III, 4, 579d.   159. *Spec.* III, 2, 578a.
160. *Spec.* III, 5, 581c.   161. *Spec.* III, 2, 578a–b.   162. *Ibid.*

that the soul finds true and profound rest: "There is silence; the sound of all that is material, external, transitory, is stilled . . . the soul sees how truly the Lord is God; . . . it has reached the Sabbath of Sabbaths."[163]

These three loves, which gather up all the aspirations of our hearts, thus reach their perfection together, but they had been advancing hand in hand, too, all along the way that leads to God.[164] Now man is "restored to himself, to his fellow-creatures and to God."[165] Charity has reformed what cupidity had deformed.[166] Ever since the moment when the sinner was converted and set anew on the way to God, charity took his natural power of loving in hand and, as a result of a long, toilsome process of purification and rectification, restored him to the likeness of God who is friendship. "Compendium of all virtue," charity is "the fulfillment of the law, the full perfection of the Gospel."[167] It is the sinner's spiritual circumcision and the Sabbath of the image that is now the likeness: "Teaching at once so complete and so concise! Doctrine of love . . . teaching all perfection!"[168]

We may conclude this first part with a summary of the key points in Aelred's doctrine of man and God, which will help to bring out the simplicity and coherence of his teaching.

The basis of Aelred's synthesis is provided by his cosmology, the elements of which, though drawn from St Augustine, were not just taken and copied cursorily but intelligently chosen and rethought before being integrated into an organic doctrinal structure. The constant use of these philosophical-theological concepts in widely different contexts and his vocabulary which was far from rigid prove that his doctrine is a unity. The basic originality of this doctrine consists primarily in the fact that it was rethought and

163. *Spec.* III, 6, 583a. 164. *Spec.* III, 2, 578b.
165. *S. Ined.*, p. 57. 166. *Ibid.*, p. 34.
167. *Spec.* II, 1, 545d. 168. *Spec.* I, 16, 520a.

experienced by a man who was intensely alive and it became his own personal property.

An analysis of the first few chapters of the *Mirror of Charity*, the treatise *On the Soul* and certain sermons of Aelred[169] may summarize his teaching as follows: all things, because they come from God, are characterized by the gift received from the Creator (*esse, species, ordo*)[170] and set in the time, place and circumstances appointed each one in the ensemble of the cosmos. Angels were created simultaneously and will never cease to be. Men appear successively, one after the other, but their souls will live on forever. Animals are created and likewise die one after the other. The whole structure of creation, by reason if its composition and end, is related to the Trinity who created it. Every creature bears some mark of the Father by its *being* which is good, is an image of the Son by its *form* which makes it beautiful, and is related to the Holy Spirit by its serviceable *purpose* which makes it of use. This relationship to God is the ultimate criterion of any creature's worth.[171]

The coherence of Aelred's doctrine is brought out by another example taken from his work. When he was created, man received from God a certain "form," namely, wisdom.[172] This is a "virtue," comes from above and is distinct from "nature." "Nature and virtue are one thing in God, two things in creatures."[173] The drama of man takes shape in this way—the "form" he received made him like to God: "The 'form' itself is the likeness to God . . . through which every creature is what it is, thanks to the giving of God's very goodness."[174] But his estrangement from God was the cause of his "deformation"; he lost wisdom: "To his cost man shed,

---

169. See especially *S. Ined.*, pp. 31–37 and 106–12.

170. This triad can also be expressed as: *natura, species, usus* (cf. *Spec.* I, 2, 506b and *S. Ined.*, p. 107). But the *natura* often denotes the *being* of a creature (cf. *S. Ined.*, pp. 34, 107 and 108, and *Epist. ad Gilbertum*, P.L. 195, col. 361–362). The *usus* is only an application of the universal law of *ordo*. Augustinian terminology on this point is variable. Cf. *Oeuvres de saint Augustin* (*Bibliothèque augustinienne*), vol. 15, p. 571.   171. *S. Ined.*, p. 140.

172. *S. Oner.* I, 363b-c.   173. *S. Oner.* VII, 391c.   174. *S. Ined.*, p. 34.

and went far off from, this 'form' of his . . . and so in truth and deed became a fool."[175] He wandered off into the land of unlikeness, which is vice and misery, while the land of likeness is all virtue and beauty.[176] The image remained in him since this was written in his nature, but the likeness, that is, wisdom, was lost. God must step in to "reform" him, if he is to come back to him.[177] The one who "reforms" God's image in us is his own Image, the Incarnate Word. He is, in fact, the Virtue of God and the Wisdom of God.[178] Through his Spirit[179] Christ will be at work on the remodelling (eruditio) of man, that is to say, his transformation in the likeness of God: "the re-education which restores our form."[180] For this purpose the Incarnate Wisdom and the Spirit made the Sacred Scriptures the source of the soul's complete "re-education," "the textbook of all our re-education,"[181] and furnished it with a doctrine that will never run short, that will suit every individual, a "fount of endless wisdom."[182] Everything, then, centers on this process of formation, deformation and reformation, and the terminology employed in the various parts of his works reveals the coherence and continuity of his thought.

On this subject the masterly sermon for the feast of Pentecost[183] deserves special mention. As regards the matter and development of Aelred's thought, it presents the essential elements of his doctrine. With magnificent simplicity it combines his teaching on creation, man, sin, redemptive incarnation, restoration by charity and spiritual friendship, relating the whole to the creative and restorative operation of the three divine Persons.

The theory of the trinitarian image in the human soul, which in the Mirror of Charity appeared simply to have been borrowed from St Augustine, comes in here again and its place in the history of the withdrawal from and return to God is underlined. The distinction

---

175. S. Oner. I, 363c.   176. S. Oner. VII, 391c.   177. S. Oner. I, 363c.
178. S. Temp. XXIV, 350d.   179. S. Ined., p. 34.   180. S. Oner. I, 363c.
181. Ibid.   182. Ibid.   183. S. Ined., pp. 106–12.

between the image and the likeness, the importance of which we have already emphasized,[184] is not only clearly defined in this sermon but is related to the divine missions. The idea of service-ableness (*utilitas*), which we called the purpose which God intended in spiritual friendship between men,[185] has also to be seen in the same plan of the economy of salvation.

Thus did Aelred understand the role of man in God's plan, and the path he has to follow to restore in himself the likeness to God who is friendship and who created human persons for union with their fellows.

In Part 2 we shall study how Aelred considered the monastic life as a way of return to God and we shall explain the principal means employed in monastic formation whose primary purpose is to achieve the progressive recovery of the divine likeness in man.

184. Cf. *supra*, p. 9.
185. *Supra*, p. 38.

PART TWO

MONASTIC LIFE
AND THE RETURN TO GOD

CHAPTER THREE

AELRED AS ABBOT:
HIS TEACHING ON THE MONASTIC LIFE

IN the organization of a monastery, as St Benedict planned it, everything rests with the abbot. Nothing of importance should be done in the monastic family without his authorization. To him is entrusted the spiritual guidance of the group of men gathered there to give themselves to the collective quest of God. He has become responsible for them, and he will leave his mark on them. The formation he gives his monks will be in accordance with the pattern of his own spiritual life. Hence, before we study Aelred's monastic ideal, we have first to consider his character as an abbot.

Father Abbot

Perhaps even more than St Bernard, whose title as Abbot of Clairvaux naturally calls to mind his widespread influence on the whole Church (which did not diminish the strong attachment he felt for his beloved valley), Aelred is pre-eminently an abbot. This is the title by which he is known to all succeeding generations, winning an indelible place in English memories.[1] He was an abbot,

1. D. Knowles, *The Monastic Order* . . ., p. 240: "No other English monk of the twelfth century so lingers in the memory." B. Pedrick, "Some Reflections on Saint Aelred of Rievaulx" in *Buckfast Abbey Chronicle* 14 (1944) 10: "Saint Aelred before everything else is a great abbot"; and he quotes from J. D. Dalgairns: "Others come down to us as holy bishops, martyrs or confessors, but Ailred was pre-eminently the Abbot of England."

and a great one, which means that he was a leader, fully aware of his spiritual and temporal responsibility, experienced in business affairs and a keen administrator. His skill in temporal affairs is unquestionably proved by the fact that under his rule Rievaulx attained great prosperity.[2] But he was more than the leader of the community he ruled; he was its teacher and guide. Whenever the spiritual welfare of his sons was involved, he always yielded to their requests: "I agree to continue and develop my subject since many, whose spiritual progress is my concern, requested it."[3] He had only one concern—to edify them in knowledge and love.[4] He devoted his life to helping them grow in God; an office of father-hood that was often painful[5] but which brought out his finest qualities of heart.

His physical appearance betrayed a delicate constitution,[6] but of such beauty as to attract.[7] His refinement may, to some extent, have been a consequence of his sojourn at the Court of Scotland, but it was probably more the reflection of a natural delicacy of mind. During the last years of his life, illness and austerities dug deep furrows in the emaciated face, of which Gilbert of Hoiland has given us this cameo: a living soul in a withered body.[8]

By scholastic standards, Aelred was not a scholar. In his youth he did indeed study in the schools of Hexham and Durham, both of good repute, but he did not remain there long enough to acquire a wide culture. Although he was not naturally attracted to specula-tion, he yet wisely esteemed learning and gave himself to it all his life. Thus he became, as Jocelin of Furness tells us, a cultured man,

2. Cf. D. Knowles, *The Monastic Order* . . ., p. 258. Also F. M. Powicke, *Vita*, Introduction, p. lxi.

3. *Epistola ad Gilbertum*, P.L. 195, 361–362.

4. *O. Past.*, 7, p. 295: *S. Oner.* I, 365.

5. *S. Oner.* IX, 397d.

6. *Vita*, p. 22.

7. *Ibid.*, p. 18.

8. P.L. 184,. 216d.

less by scholastic studies than by the judicious and constant exercise of his natural powers, which were especially keen.[9]

It is chiefly his personality that interests us. Gentleness, courtesy and a goodness bordering on tenderness[10] all combined to make his temperament affective to such a degree that it seems to be its chief trait. He had by nature a great gift of fellow-feeling, so that he found "nothing so desirable, so pleasant, so spiritually useful . . . as friendship."[11] He had an intense relish for the joys of friendship.[12] To this affective nature, however, was joined a sense of moderation, a practical wisdom that made him patient with and understanding of every human weakness;[13] a born conciliator, he preferred to achieve harmony by using mildness rather than to set up divisions by opposition, or to refute with bitterness. While he was firm in his defense of the interests and ideals of the Order, he seldom displayed the zeal, often biting, of St Bernard. He was not, by nature, a controversialist or a pamphleteer; he preferred always to remain the patient leader or the silent partner. Needless to say, gentleness such as his was often put to the test in his large community where so many diverse and unpolished characters rubbed shoulders.

He was the father of them all: this explains all his behavior. Abbot Aelred has left us a remarkable document that deserves to be better known, read and pondered. The *Pastoral Prayer* is "one of the finest writings that express the piety of medieval monasticism."[14] In this prayer we can grasp the depth of affection and

9. *Vita S. Waldeni*, in *Acta Sanctorum*, III Augusti, t. I, edit. Palme, Paris, 1867: 258c.

10. *Ibid.*, 258c-d.   11. *Am.*, Prologue, 659a, p. 2.

12. *Epistola ad Gilbertum*, P.L. 195, col. 361-362: *Animus proinde meus amoris impetus sequens . . . in ipsum tuae mentis sinum se totum infundit. . . ut ex spiritus tui participatione meus spiritus renovetur . . .* In *Spec.* I, 34, 539-546 Aelred expresses the sorrow he felt at the death of his friend Simon.

13. Jocelin of Furness, *Vita S. Waldeni*, in *Acta Sanctorum*, III Augusti, t. I, 258d: *Erat nihilominus supra omnes coaetaneos suos ecclesiae praelatus mansuetus et patiens, et infirmitatibus corporum et morum aliorum valde compatiens.*

14. A. Wilmart, "L'Oraison pastorale de l'Abbé Aelred" in *Rev. Bén.* 41 (1929) 74.

devotion Aelred had for his monks. It is sufficient to listen to him pray to be convinced of his sincerity and sensitiveness of soul.

He knew that his office required a special gift of discernment of spirits. Souls differ greatly and so do their qualities.[15] Consequently he begs the Lord to give him wisdom: "To be at my side and share my labors and efforts, make me her spokesman, put order into my thoughts, words, deeds, decisions; may all this, as it shall please you, give honor to your name, do good to my brethren, make for my soul's salvation."[16]

Whenever the welfare of those whom he looks upon and loves as his children is involved, he asks God for the grace to give himself generously: "You know well how great is my love for them, how I feel for them, how very fond I am of them."[17] "My will is that all your gifts to me be at their disposal absolutely. I will spend myself unreservedly on their behalf . . . ; all that I am, my life, views, understanding, all be at their service."[18]

An abbot has the duty—difficult and arduous in St Benedict's opinion[19]—of adapting himself to different temperaments. The desire dearest to Aelred's heart was to belong to every one of them: "Grant me to accommodate myself to the character, ways, disposition, gifts, shortcomings of each; to do as circumstances demand, and as you see best."[20]

Walter Daniel bears witness to the fact that Aelred's manner of acting was in keeping with the desires he expressed in this prayer. Towards a cleric of particularly unstable character, who was restless in the monastery and eventually ran off into the woods, Aelred showed himself so long-suffering that he succeeded in leading him back, now at peace, to the "haven of salvation." He persevered faithfully and died in Aelred's arms.[21]

---

15. *S. Oner.* XXIX, 485c-d.   16. *O. Past.*, 6, p. 294.

17. *O. Past.*, 8, p. 295.   18. *O. Past.*, 7, p. 294.

19. "Let him understand also what a difficult and arduous task he has undertaken: ruling souls and adapting himself to a variety of characters" (*Rule, op. cit.*, p. 11).

20. *O. Past.*, 7, p. 295.   21. *Vita*, pp. 24–25.

Guided by wise discretion and filled with humble charity, his heart played the leading part in winning such victories: "You know, Lord, my intention is not so much to be their superior as to lovingly help them and humbly serve them; to be, at their side, one of them."[22]

His self-forgetfulness is expressed in these touching words: "Grant them, Lord, the grace to ever think and feel towards me, your servant and theirs for your sake, as best serves their spiritual welfare; let them love and fear me, but only so far as you see is for their good."[23]

No analysis or paraphrase, we must admit, could have revealed to us Aelred's beauty of soul as these words do—and so spontaneously. We must needs let him speak for himself and listen to this Good Shepherd telling us of his desires and his concerns, and praying for peace for his flock: "May they, Lord, thanks to your Spirit's influence, live at peace, each and all, and with me; may they be well-behaved, kindly disposed; may they obey, help and bear with one another."[24]

A unique feature of monastic life at Rievaulx was the spontaneous and informal dialogues Aelred had with his monks. Walter Daniel tells us—what we could in any case gather from Aelred's *Mirror of Charity* and *On Spiritual Friendship*—that when he was novice-master the novices would come to him, singly or in small groups, for an impromptu talk on spiritual things. Later when he became abbot, Aelred continued this practice and it became a regular feature of the last years of his life, when he lived in the cell beside the infirmary: "Twenty or thirty at a time, the monks came to talk together of the spiritual delights of Holy Scripture and the observances of the Order. There was nobody to say to them: 'Away with you. Don't touch the abbot's bed.' They walked and lay about his bed and talked with him as children chatter to their mother."[25]

22. *O. Past.*, 8, p. 295.   23. *O. Past.*, 9, p. 296.
24. *O. Past.*, 8, p. 296.   25. *Vita*, p. 40.

What more homely and delightful picture of Aelred as the father and teacher of his monks could be found!

Each religious house has its own spirit which gives it its distinctive character, and very often it can be traced to the influence of an abbot, who over a period of years gave his monks that particular character, that particular orientation. Now what, we may ask, was the spirit of Rievaulx? What had the abbot wanted it to be? How did the monks themselves consider their monastic family? There is a fine passage in Walter Daniel's *Life* of Aelred where the resemblance of Rievaulx to its abbot is portrayed. The ideal of the monastery was to offer a welcome to everyone as a "Mother of Mercy." Rievaulx' singular glory was that it showed understanding and compassion towards the weak and needy.[26] Such was the spirit of Rievaulx, a faithful copy of that of its abbot.

The Straight Way

Aelred saw the course of mankind's destiny as a curve which first sloped downwards, then upwards. By an act of his free will,[27] man turned away from his Creator and was caught in a tedious and painful vicious circle.[28] He was restored to his true nature by another act of his will,[29] when, under the influence of its Exemplar, the image was set anew towards God: "It is clear, if I mistake not, that while pride means consciously withdrawing one's affection . . . from God and withering up selfishly, to the detriment of God's likeness, humility means deliberately drawing close to God, recovering the created likeness of God."[30]

26. *Vita,* p. 37.

27. *Spec.* I, 4, 508c; I, 12, 516b.

28. *Spec.* I, 15, 519c; I, 22, 526a.

29. *Spec.* I, 10, 514a.

30. *Spec.* I, 8, 512b.

At the center of this history of liberation and gratuitous salvation is God, the center of gravity of every creature, the pole of attraction and the sole resting place of the rational creature called to divine likeness.[31] This study of mankind is of particular interest since it reveals to us the mysterious meaning of our nature marked with the divine seal, and the profound significance of our aspirations and our pangs of anguish.[32] The return to God is the very problem confronting man. In rejecting God, a man denies himself[33]—surely a traditional theme in the religious thought of all ages. This is not the place to give even a brief summary of the development of an idea which in itself is an epitome of religion. Finding it thus presented in various contexts helps us to gain some idea of its importance and tends to emphasize the originality with which it was engrafted in the Christian presentation of the history of salvation. While it is necessary to take account of the undeniable influence of Neoplatonism on a considerable number of Christian thinkers, and these not by any means the least,[34] it must be recognized that in the Christian context the idea acquires a quite new depth of meaning.

As described by Aelred, the return to God places us in a specifically Christian atmosphere. At the root of his doctrinal synthesis, the dogma of creation governs all the relationships of creatures vis-à-vis God and is incompatible with any form of pantheism.[35] The Christian mysteries, by their absolute transcendence and internal

31. *Spec.* I, 2, 507a.   32. *Spec.* I, 22, 525b.

33. *Spec.* I, 4, 508d; I, 7, 512a. Cf. N. Berdiaeff, *Un nouveau Moyen Age*, Paris, 1930, p. 106: *Là où il n'y a plus de Dieu, il n'y a plus d'homme.*

34. Without going so far as to claim, as does Castren (*Barnhard von Clairvaux, Zur Typologie des mittelalterlichen Menschen*, Lund, 1938), that not only the main lines of St Bernard's thought are Neoplatonic, but that his *caritas* is not the *agape* of the Gospels, we can, however, subscribe to the opinion of Dom Déchanet (in *Saint Bernard Théologien*, p. 77): "I think Bernard read . . . some, indeed much, of Plato."

35. Etienne Gilson has underlined "the essential role which the doctrine of the image—in other words, the basically Jewish and Christian concept of creation—plays in Cistercian mysticism." By reason of which Christianity

connection, bring out still more and in an irreducible fashion the true nature of this religion of salvation in which human persons and God himself have a free part to play. There is a radical difference between Platonism and Christianity: man does not, and cannot, effect his restoration by his own natural powers.[36] For a Christian there can be no such thing as self-redemption; it is Another who frees him from the slavery of sin.[37] Men are brought to God by Christ, the conqueror of Satan and sin and death.[38] The mystery of iniquity makes way for the mystery of Christ. Christ is our paschal victim.[39] The unique and indispensable mediator, he carries on his work through the mystery of the Church, the community of salvation.[40] Through her and in her is accomplished the journey to God whose highest mystery is to be Love.[41]

The return to God, seen in this light, lies at the very heart of Christianity. To detach ourselves from sin[42] in order to be attached to Christ, whom the Church gives us, is to take a personal step towards union of love with a personal God, an economy of salvation that restores the fallen human race. This is the paschal mystery,[43]

---

avoids the error of pantheism: "Augustine, Gregory of Nyssa, Dionysius, Maximus, Erigenus, Bernard and so many others besides, would be turned into pantheists if this central doctrine of the image were taken out of their teaching" (in *Beiträge für die Geschichte der Phil. und Theol. des M.A.*, Suppt. Bd. III, Münster, 1935, pp. 193–94).

36. See R. Arnou, art. "Platonisme des Pères" in *Dict. Théol. Cath.* XII (1935) col. 2368.

37. Luke 2:21–22.   38. See *supra*, p. 19.

39. 1 Cor 5:7. Cf. *S. Ined.*, p. 95.   40. *S. Ined.*, p. 40. *S. Temp.* I, 218a-b.

41. *Spec.* I, 1, 505c.

42. For Neoplatonists conversion signified estrangement and separation from matter. See A. Arnou, "Le platonisme des Pères" in *Dict. Théol. Cath.* XII (1935) col. 2364. Dom J. M. Déchanet finds this nuance in Saint Bernard: "Aux sources de la pensée philosophique de Saint Bernard" in *Saint Bernard Théologien*, pp. 65 and 72.

43. See J. Daniélou, "Cathéchèse pascale et retour au Paradis" in *La Maison-Dieu*, no. 45, pp. 99–119.

the deep-reaching significance and life-giving wealth of which is happily being rediscovered in our day.[44]

In the Cistercian school of the twelfth century special importance is laid upon the spiritual enterprise of the soul's return to God, with the pains and joys it involves because of the painful conflict[45] in which the soul is both the scene of operation and the prize at stake. These writers, starting with a clearly conceived anthropology,[46] aimed primarily at describing the soul's ascent to God by way of charity,[47] and they had greater interest than others[48] in the psychological aspect of the experiences[49] of a soul in its quest for God.[50]

In this quest for God Aelred showed himself a spiritual master. The monastic life, in fact, is, and ought to be, nothing but a sincere striving for the perfection of the Christian life. It cannot, therefore, be esoteric either in relation to human nature or in relation to the Christian ideal. For Aelred it is the straight way for returning to God[51] through the victory of charity: "Consequently one who, in his longing to reach the peak of perfection, has freely dedicated

44. See *Vie Spir.* 94 (1956) 317, for a review by I. H. Dalmais of H. Oster's book, *Le grand dessein de Dieu dans la pastorale et la prédication,* Paris, 1955.

45. *Spec.* I, 9, 513b.

46. See *supra,* beginning of Chapter I.

47. A. Le Bail, *Les traités de la charité dans l'Ordre de Cîteaux* (unpublished), t. I, pp. 4, 6, 20 and 133.

48. We say "greater interest than others", but needless to say, this flair for psychology was not the exclusive privilege of the Cistercians. It revealed itself in the school of Chartres as well, in William de Conches. See. P. Michaud-Quantin, "La classification des puissances de l'âme" in *Rev. M.A. Lat.* 5 (1949) 17.

49. P. Delfgaauw, in *Saint Bernard Théologien,* p. 246, n. 2: "For Saint Bernard the steps (of this ascent) are experiences."

50. It is true to say that these *gradus* did exist and will exist in other writers (Neoplatonists, the Greek Fathers, St Augustine, the Victorines, Franciscans...), but the Cistercian school described them with greater detail and endeavored to show how these steps differed and tried to express in symbols the mysterious transitions—*transitus, excessus*—those interior changes brought about in man by the action of God.

51. *S. Temp.* VI, 247b.

himself to a particular way of life, must, first of all, keep love, the objective and purpose of all his striving, ceaselessly in view. Love does not merely make possible the greatest intimacy with God, closest union with him, it is all perfection. Secondly, he must with invincible generosity fight his way along the whole course mapped out by his vow or profession."[52]

Aelred's monastic doctrine, therefore, is primarily a doctrine of salvation. The Christian flies from the world and withdraws into solitude with a high end in view, that of securing his salvation. The traditional concept of monastic life, the principal motive that led the first hermits to the desert, was the salvation of their souls.[53] Far from savoring of selfishness, this withdrawal from the world proclaimed the primacy of the spiritual over the temporal and the monk's strong conviction of the one thing necessary. Passages can be cited from Aelred to prove that this ideal remained unchanged in the twelfth century: the monastic life was regarded primarily as a means, the most excellent of all means, to lead fallen man back to God. The Abbot of Rievaulx explicitly pointed out the difficulty confronting all men of effecting this necessary return and the relative ease offered by the cloister to those who desired to fix themselves deliberately on the way to God.[54]

The world bristles with dangers. Just as people in the Middle Ages, living in a country frequently embroiled in wars, protected themselves in strong castles or behind city walls, so Christians collect and join forces in various "cities." Some withdraw into the

---

52. *Spec.* III, 36, 613b-c.

53. See *Apophthegmata Patrum*, P.G. 65; *Arsenius* 1, 87; *Hierax* 1, 231; *Macarius Aegypt.* 27, 273-41, 281. J. Leclercq, *La vie parfaite*, p. 10: "The Fathers of the monastic life in the early centuries, and St Benedict in particular, did not distinguish between the requirements for perfection and those for salvation."

54. D. Knowles, *The Monastic Order . . .*, p. 220, remarks that souls wishing to attain salvation found at Rievaulx the answer to their great question: "What must I do that I may possess eternal life?" It was: "Enter here: live as we do; this do, and thou shalt live."

"city" of marriage, where they are protected from evil passions. Others want a still more impregnable stronghold: Cîteaux provides them with such a one. "Our way of life is a strongly fortified city, its battlements and towers the wise observances that shelter us on all sides from the surprise attacks of our enemy. . . . What a battlement poverty is! . . . Silence is such a tower. . . . Yes, our observances enable us to tower over vice . . . keep us strong to meet the enemy's assault."[55]

Elsewhere the arduous enterprise of salvation is compared by Aelred to a dangerous crossing of a rough sea: "The sea that keeps us from God is the world that passes. . . . While some drown in this sea, others cross it." The man who wants to make a safe crossing has need of a ship; marriage is a "rather fragile vessel," the monastic way of life, "a fine, seaworthy ship."[56]

The obstacle hindering our return to God is sin, which has raised a wall between God and us. The man who embraces monastic discipline storms this barrier across his path: "Sharp steel alone will enable us to break down this wall; the sharp steel of penance. . . . It is for the steel of abstinence to destroy impurity, that of poverty to do away with avarice, that of silence to remove quarreling."[57]

Even when we are willing and ready to undertake the work of restoration, a thick cloud, hanging over and obscuring the path, puts us astray: "Ignorance is the cloud that only too often blinds us to our duties." But the Lord has provided us with a torch, his own Word. Sacred Scripture is the light that must guide our going to him who calls out to us here on earth: *Transite ad me*—Approach me.[58]

The Cistercian way is, then, a secure way of salvation: is it the best? We know how zealously St Bernard became "God's fisherman,"[59] attracting and urging men to the monastic life, to Clairvaux. "To Bernard's way of thinking, the Cistercian life is the only way

55. *S. Temp.* II, 221a-b.
56. *S. Temp.* XIX, 316–317b.
57. *Ibid.,* 317d.
58. *Ibid.,* 318a.
59. A. Dimier, *Saint Bernard "pêcheur de Dieu"*, Paris, 1953.

that leads surely to salvation."[60] We have to admit that, preoccupied with this idea, he expressed it so boldly and categorically that it often disconcerts us.[61] His sincerity cannot be doubted; his very vehemence betokens his deep conviction. "Where could men save their souls better than at Cîteaux, which Bernard looked upon as a school of sanctity absolutely unique of its kind, where monks were able to lead a life as angelic as possible on earth? From this position to that of regarding the Order of Cîteaux as the sole way of saving one's soul was but a step, and St Bernard seems to have taken this step more than once. There is a temptation to think that sometimes he was not far from believing that outside Cîteaux there is no salvation."[62]

Aelred was careful to avoid such pious exaggerations. If he did not preach the almost exclusive excellence of the Cistercian life as eloquently as Bernard, he nevertheless shared his appreciation of the beauty of the vocation that was his, and he defended and propagated it in England.[63] He did not, perhaps, have Bernard's success or power in attracting souls by an appeal to the mystical life,[64] but he stamped Rievaulx with the spirit of peace and compassionate charity, for which many souls yearned and the comfort of which they appreciated.

The way leading to God in the religious state is a straight and sure one, yet a man travels it only step by step and at the cost of prolonged labor. After deliberately orienting himself towards God alone by

60. A. Fliche, "Saint Bernard et la société civile de son temps" in *Bernard de Clairvaux*, Paris and Aiguebelle, 1953, p. 359.

61. A. Dimier, "Saint Bernard et le droit en matière de Transitus" in *Rev. Mabillon* 43 (1953) 48–52.

62. *Ibid.*, p. 80.

63. Such was his purpose in one of his very first works: *Un court traité d'Aelred sur l'étendue et le but de la profession monastique*, published by A. Wilmart in *Rev. Asc. Myst.* 23 (1947) 259–73.

64. D. Knowles, *The Monastic Order . . .* , p. 223, remarks that it has not been sufficiently noted by the historians of monasticism how new such an appeal was in monastic life at that time.

monastic conversion, the renunciation of the world that Aelred likens to a second, spiritual birth,[65] a monk has to accept and undergo a painful purification, which will permit the Lord to fulfill, at least from time to time, his soul's yearning: at the moment chosen by his love, he will come to visit him by contemplation, which is a foretaste of the happiness of the heavenly homeland.[66] Aelred thought of these stages in terms of the chosen people's journey from Egypt to the promised land. In the inspired narrative of this people's destiny, a spiritual man is able to read, with the aid of allegory, not only the outlines of the history of salvation, but also the soul's various experiences in its quest of God.[67]

Exodus from Egypt

The exodus is a constantly recurring theme in monastic literature, which is fed by the patristic tradition and lives by the liturgy. It is frequently applied to monastic conversion, the step taken by a man, who, called to the perfect life, leaves the world and sets out on a pilgrimage to a promised land as alluring as it is distant and mysterious.[68] It is no light undertaking, for a man does not quit Egypt unhindered, nor break with the world without running into much opposition. Drawing, no doubt, on his own experience, Aelred realistically recalls all these obstacles and pains: "Once a man makes known his decision to forsake the world and seek God,

65. *S. Temp.* V, 239a: St Benedict is our Father: "for in Christ Jesus, through the Gospel, he gave us birth." Walter Daniel says the same of Aelred: "who gave me birth through the Gospel of God into the life of Saint Benedict" (*Vita*, p. 2).

66. *S. Temp.* VII, 328b; *S. Oner* XXXI, 247d.

67. This is fully in line with all Christian tradition. Cf. J. Guillet, *Thèmes bibliques*, Paris, 1951, p. 21: "The old Testament is indispensable for interpreting the central fact of Christianity. . . . Christians are fond of going to this Old Testament history in order to understand better their own experiences. The symbol of the Exodus and the journey through the desert holds pride of place."

68. *S. Temp.* VII, 247d.

there is no end of objections, claims, cries. What, can you leave us? Is your father to be neglected in his old age? Must your widowed mother be left destitute? . . . Leave us like this? Are we to part?"[69]

There is a note of urgency in Aelred's voice when he is encouraging souls to cross the Red Sea and strike out into the desert, for this is the real crux. The sincerity of a man's conversion is proved and measured by the genuineness of his renunciation of the world. Aelred frequently returns to this point and urges it with an insistence that reveals his conviction, a Gospel conviction besides, that we cannot approach God without detachment. He considers this separation from the world as the indispensable condition of success.[70] It is idle to think that we can fly through the stages; we only go to God step by step.[71] If there has been no true conversion, there can be no real purification of the soul: "Whoever would reach this highest degree must first make a thorough job of the two earlier steps (conversion and purification) . . . . Turning to God must be neither half-hearted nor feigned . . . a case of not fully forsaking everything."[72]

Aelred, however, teaches the generous monk that he loses nothing in forsaking these things. In place of worldly riches, he will receive spiritual ones; in detaching himself from material goods, he will break the bonds that prevent him from climbing "unburdened the ladder that leads to God."[73]

Active Life in the Desert

After quitting Egypt, a land of darkness, the monk must prepare himself for the journey through the desert, a place of trials. By way of solitude, weariness, the tediousness of plodding on, God works

---

69. *S. Temp.* XXI, 332b-c.

70. *S. Temp.* XVI, 301c. Cf. XXI, 331b-c; XXV, 353c; *S. Oner.* XVIII, 434d; *Inst.*, p. 179.

71. *S. Temp.* XXI, 328a.   72. *Ibid.*, 328b-c.   73. *Ibid.*, 331b.

on the soul, stimulating its desire for the promised land and preparing it for the full enjoyment of it by indispensable purifications. In monastic spirituality the desert represents the entire period of necessary toil which is the ordinary prelude to intimate union with God.[74] The active life involves the whole burden of suffering and struggle which prepares and leads the soul to the rest of contemplation.[75] Just as the Jewish people in the desert underwent many tribulations, which for some of them proved to be an occasion of triumph and a source of blessings, for others a stumbling block on which they were broken,[76] so monks will meet on their path all the varied and dangerous enemies symbolized by Amalech, Sehon, Og and Madian.[77]

The first disposition required in the monk who wants to follow St Benedict, the new Moses, through the desert of this life, is that he sincerely give himself to God. As Aelred has just emphasized, there are some who do not pursue their conversion to its logical conclusion. They claim to forsake the world, yet remain attached to it. Men who were poor in the world, now want to "live at their ease" in the monastery and consider it their right to have in the cloister what they did not even possess before their profession.[78] Aelred rightly pins little hope on such conversions carried out so hesitantly and half-heartedly.[79] If a man really wants to succeed in the long and difficult stages that lie ahead, he must from the beginning have made up his mind to carry through this adventure courageously. The Abbot of Rievaulx looks upon generosity at the start as one of the conditions of success: "Whoever forsakes the world and goes about his conversion in a lazy, half-hearted and careless fashion makes, even if his former life was not very disordered, scarcely any headway towards tranquillity of conscience and the liberty that comes of love."[80]

74. *S. Ined.*, p. 63.
76. *S. Ined.*, p. 63.
78. *S. Ined.*, p. 168.
80. *Spec.* II, 21, 570b.

75. *S. Ined.*, p. 174.
77. *Ibid.*
79. *S. Temp* XXI, 328c.

Aelred knows the effective means for making progress. He requires the soul to comply in the first place with three conditions, symbolized by the three days' journey of Israel into a parched and harsh country,[81] namely, forsaking the world, leaving one's sins and giving up one's self-will:[82] "Whoever really leaves Egypt fulfills these three conditions. In other words, he not merely makes an external renunciation of riches, and does not confine himself to daily and habitually refusing to desire them, he even keeps himself in God's presence, free from all covetousness and ambition."[83]

At times many, disconcerted by the wanderings up and down the desert—God's unpredictable ways which follow a pattern not our own—feel the crushing weight of discouragement. Such souls, tried by weariness or dejected by dryness, are reminded by Aelred of God's ways of dealing with his chosen people: "The Israelites . . . once they crossed the Red Sea, so little deserved to be strengthened by the food of angels, they were led to the waters of Mara and put to the test. . . . You left Egypt behind, passed dryshod through this world's towering waves, but only to be brought to the waters of Mara, of Bitterness, to . . . learn by your own experience the truth of those words of the Gospel, 'How narrow the road that leads on to life'."[84]

The Abbot of Rievaulx is grieved to observe the tepidity, or worse still, the falling away of some of his monks. There are some, he says, who outwardly appear good but are rotten within.[85] Though religious should shine like stars, some are more like charcoal in their lack of luster.[86] What a distressing sight it is to see monks who, after a sincere conversion, relax their first fervor and fall bit by bit![87] What a sad thing it is to behold some seniors slipping ever deeper into mediocrity with the years![88] Woe to those who lag behind on the way and trust in a false security: "Some . . . with grave faults

81. Ex 15:22. S. Temp. V, 241c.   82. S. Temp. V, 241d.
83. S. Temp. V, 242b.   84. Spec. II, 15, 560d–561a.
85. S. Oner. XI, 405d.   86. S. Oner. X, 404c.
87. S. Oner. XXX, 494b.   88. S. Ined., pp. 167–68.

to atone for, make profession of this penitential way of life . . . yet become so idle and lazy they despise even the most indispensable observances."[89]

Aelred reminds everyone of the necessity for pressing on. Salvation is not achieved without man's cooperation; there is no mysticism without asceticism: "He who shirks spiritual warfare in this life is no better than a beast."[90] The monk who has no longer the desire to fight on becomes the wretched slave of his vices. Aelred took a secret literary delight in sketching, as he did on several occasions, the portrait of monks who are tormented and disturbed by their undisciplined passions.[91] In these descriptions he was served by the keen eye he had for observing psychological phenomena, though he was also following the taste writers of his time and race had for satirizing certain traditional figures.[92] Some monks, no doubt fearing the tediousness of solitude and silence, are all ears for every scrap of news: "Such devoted collectors of rumor rake in enough to keep their minds busy with all the affairs of the realm, even during the psalmody itself."[93] The monk who is so absorbed with these foolish interests in the midst of the peace of the cloister is no better than a gad-about.[94] Others are given to gluttony. Descriptions of the excesses of this vice form one of the literary genres of ancient and medieval ascetical literature. The Abbot of Rievaulx alludes to the exaggerated lengths to which some monks can go in this matter, when they expect the superior to have the quality of the food correspond to the liturgical solemnity of the day and the number of courses proportioned to the number of lessons at Vigils.[95]

But sorrow and deception are not the only lot of an abbot who guides souls on their journey. What a comfort and joy it is to him

---

89. *S. Oner.* XXIV, 463d.   90. *S. Temp.* XV, 294d.
91. *S. Oner.* XV, 424c; *S. Ined.*, p. 164.
92. See J. de Ghellinck, *L'essor de la littérature au XIIe siècle*, t. II, p. 306.
93. *Spec.* II, 24, 573d; *Inst.*, p. 178.   94. *S. Ined.*, p. 69.
95. *Spec.* II, 4, 549b.

to see souls advancing through the desert, those who had once been wolves now become lambs, and the proud attaining to the simplicity of the children of God![96]

Entry into the Promised Land

The desert is a place we pass through, not a place in which we settle down permanently. The Jews, freed from Egypt, were en route for the land promised them by Almighty God. Monks, too, at the call of this same God, who draws them on and is so demanding, have left the world and its good things, and set out for the land promised them if they are faithful. The toil and struggle, which mark the stages of their wayfaring, are really only a purification, a re-creation,[97] a preparation for a more intimate possession of God. When a soul has been detached and purified from earthly things, it enjoys the sweetness of heavenly things.[98] The active life is only the normal prelude to the contemplative life. It is important to avoid considering these as separated from each other in water-tight compartments. On the contrary, they will alternate in the same soul, depending on obedience or divine attraction,[99] and they can live together at peace[100] in the same monastic community, where, in fact, the very necessary diversity of function safeguards the harmonious unity of the whole. Martha and Mary are meant to live in the same house, not isolated from, or opposed to, each other. The Lord will have both of them carry out their respective functions, which are complementary, not contradictory, to each other.[101] Following the Rule of St Benedict, who wisely prescribed a balanced distribution of monastic occupations, monks are to unite in their

96. *S. Temp.* I, 216a-b.   97. *S. Ined.,* p. 62.   98. *S. Oner.* II, 371a.
99. *S. Temp.* XVII, 307a.   100. *Inst.* 28, pp. 198–99.
101. *S. Temp.* XVII, 308a.

lives the practice of the *corporalia* and the *spiritualia* and are to be now Martha, now Mary.[102]

Whether it has journeyed by winding roads or more direct routes, the soul arrives at the Jordan at the moment God judges opportune. In front of it stretches out the promised land of contemplation. This experience is not the final stage of the spiritual life; it is but a fore-taste of the true country of heaven, yet it is a Sabbath, an earnest of the everlasting Sabbath. A monk's trials are by no means over; he has still to press on and overcome other obstacles. Moses is no longer there to guide and encourage the people on their travels. His mission is ended; Josue takes his place.[103] In place of St Benedict too, another Josue succeeds (in Hebrew *Jesus* and *Josue* are identical). It is now Jesus himself who will lead us into the promised land and aid us in overcoming our final enemies symbolized by Jericho, Hai and the five petty kings. The monk who desires to enjoy the sweet-ness of contemplation must fight against acedia, depression and all pride's satellites,[104] and secure certain conditions without which there could be no true or flourishing contemplative life. In the first place God loves a solitary soul, in the sense that he draws it into solitude and there speaks to it intimately. "Let the soul remain alone, then, quietly listening to Christ and speaking to him."[105] The man who talks much does not hear God, and so Aelred repeats the advice of the Fathers of the Desert: "Be still, quiet, enduring."[106] In solitude and silence the soul is to grow in peace and remain in joy. Contemplation cannot co-exist with any form of commotion, hence "it is not for those who live in monasteries to be burdened with cares"[107] which would turn their life into a dissolvent activism. Joy, which is God's gift to generous souls,[108] should be the very

---

102. On this interesting topic see the article by C. Dumont: "L'équilibre humain de la vie cistercienne d'après le Bienheureux Aelred de Rievaulx" in *Collectanea O.C.R.* 18 (1956) 177–89.

103. *S. Ined.*, p. 68. 104. *Ibid.*, p. 69. 105. *Inst.* 5, p. 181.

106. *Ibid.*, 4, p. 179, Cf. *Apophthegmata*, P.G. 65, col. 87. *Arsenius*, 2: *Fuge, tace, quiesce.*

107. *Ibid.*, 28, p. 199. 108. *S. Ined.*, p. 71.

atmosphere of the contemplative life.[109] The soul whom God visits is full of tranquillity and at the same time full of expectancy. It looks upon the things of the world as "mere smoke" or an "unsubstantial shadow," and reaches eagerly out towards the joys of heaven;[110] yet it lives in peace, in a most sacred state which it will be the "chief object of the soul's endeavors to acquire and preserve."[111]

The School of Christ

In the twelfth century, the expression "the school of Christ" (*Schola Christi*) seems to have maintained, at least in monastic circles, the two connotations that characterized the historical development of the word *schola*.[112] It denotes the company of soldiers who enlisted voluntarily in the service of Christ, to quote the phrase used by St Benedict in the prologue of his Rule: "whoever has a mind to fight for the true King, Christ our Lord . . . (in) the school of the Lord's service."[113] Thus the Great Exordium of Cîteaux describes the Order as a school of Christ.[114] In this sense the word suggests the teaching given in a monastery where Christ is the principal Master, an idea so dear to St Bernard: "You are Master and Lord, you who teach on earth and reign in heaven."[115] The cloister is a school,[116] which offers an education preferable to the science of the schools. In the twelfth century particularly the phrase "the school

109. *S. Ined.*, p. 69.   110. *Ibid.*, p. 174.   111. *Inst.* 7, p. 183.

112. See G. Pare, A. Brunet, P. Trumblay, *La Renaissance du XIIe siècle, les écoles et l'enseignement*, p. 59, n. 3.

113. ". . . to do battle under the Lord Christ the true King . . ." (*Rule, op. cit.*, p. 1); ". . . a school for the service of the Lord" (*loc. cit.*, p. 5.)

114. *Exordium Magnum Ordinis Cisterciensis*, dist. I, cap. 2, P.L. 185, 998a.

115. *Sermones in diversis* XL, 1; P.L. 183, 647a.

116. E. Gilson, *The Mystical Theology of St Bernard*, p. 63: "The Cistercians entertained no merely scholastic conception of the monastic life, but rather, on the other hand, a monastic conception of the scholastic life. They reduced the School to the Cloister."

of Christ" almost invariably included an overtone of opposition to intellectual studies, which were considered too worldly. The following remark of Philip de Harvengt, a Premonstratensian, to one of his friends, for instance, illustrates this preference of the monks: "Happy, not he who follows the lectures of Anselm (of Laon) . . . but the man who has you, Lord, for master."[117] And we know with what indignant zeal and striking courage such an enthusiastic supporter of "the school of Christ" as Rupert of Deutz opposed the "novelties" issuing from Laon and Paris.[118]

The same tendency was apparent at Rievaulx where, nevertheless, were to be found at this time monks who had attended the schools —the *litterati* as they were called. We catch an echo of it in the conclusion of a sermon by Walter Daniel: "Christ, our Master, did not teach grammar, rhetoric, dialectics, in his school; he taught humility, meekness and justice."[119] Aelred, too, speaks in a similar strain. He repeatedly acknowledged that he had never been educated in the fashion of the schools:[120] "scarcely able to read,"[121] he added with a touch of humor that he was a graduate "of the kitchen[122] rather than the schools."[123] Besides he showed no taste for the subtleties of speculation and gladly left to others the pleasure of disputations and controversies; "Let those skilled in arguing such matters settle it."[124] He even found fault with those who, instead of following the counsels of the Holy Fathers in questions of chant, preferred "the senseless trumpery provided by some schoolman or other."[125] St Bernard naturally approved of this attitude and the man

117. *Epist. 7 ad Joannem*, P.L. 203, 59a.

118. *In Regulam S. Benedicti*, I, P.L. 170, 480–83.

119. This sermon, with three others, follows the *Centum Sententiae* of Walter Daniel in a manuscript in the John Rylands Library. F. M. Powicke quotes it in the Introduction to his *Vita Ailredi*, p. xxvi.

120. He did, however, attend the schools. See *supra*, p. 60.

121. *S. Oner.* I, 365c; *Epist. S. Bernardi*, P.L. 195, 501–502.

122. An allusion to his office as steward at the Royal Court of Scotland.

123. *Epist. S. Bernardi*, P.L. 195, 501–502.

124. *Jesu*, P.L. 184, 856a.   125. *Spec.* II, 23, 572b.

who was responsible for the *Mirror of Charity* cannot but have rejoiced at the thought of a work written in the "school of the Holy Spirit." Many things, indeed, are revealed "beneath the shady trees" which would be sought in vain "in the schools."[126] The Abbot of Rievaulx openly admitted to his monks that his most profound knowledge, his spiritual learning, was derived, not from scholastic studies, but from the Lord.[127]

A monastery is a school that imparts not merely knowledge but also the stimulus to act on that knowledge. The aim and endeavor of the *schola disciplinae* is to bring one's knowledge and one's way of life into harmony:[128] "school of the apprentices rather than of the students of Christ, for in that school the exercises are acts."[129] Man's re-education, that is, his re-formation by wisdom, is its aim. Knowledge alone could not achieve this, but *eruditio*, in the sense it has in Christian tradition, involves the twofold signification of instruction and formative discipline.[130] Without asceticism it is vain to hope for the restoration of fallen nature.[131] There has to be a building up[132] in faith, hope and charity: "The whole of re-education, all re-forming our deformity, consists in three things—faith, hope and charity."[133] The re-education is Wisdom itself who made the Scriptures the "source of all re-education.[134]"

In this school of Christ learning and living cannot normally be

---

126. *Epist. S. Bernardi*, P.L. 195, 501–502.

127. *S. Oner.* I, 365c.

128. P.L. 176, 877b: *in disciplina ut laudabiliter vivens, mores cum scientia componat* (attributed to Hugh of Saint-Victor).

129. E. Gilson, *The Mystical Theology of St Bernard*, p. 67.

130. These two meanings were to be found together in the Divine Office on 7 March 1956: *mira eruditione clarificas* (Collect for the feast of St Thomas Aquinas) and *ut salutaribus jejuniis* eruditi (Collect for 4th ferial after 3rd Sunday of Lent).

131. Cf. *Thesaurus linguae latinae, Eruditio: sensu strictiore ap. Christianos: de ea eruditione quae puniendo, castigando . . . paratur.* Rufinus: *disciplina vel eruditio est institutio quaedam cum labore adhibita animae.* Augustinus: *per molestas eruditio.*

132. *S. Oner.* I, 365b.   133. *Ibid.*, 363c.   134. *Ibid.*

separated. The quest for knowledge, which is here a theology,[135] is not satisfied with purely intellectual speculation, but aims at a true spiritual experience[136] of, and contact with, God, which brings joy, and expresses itself in prayer.[137] It requires the soul to be attentive and receptive: "Harken, my son, to the precepts of your Master, and incline the ear of your heart."[138] The abbot, in the name of Christ,[139] is the master: he teaches and the monastic family listens. We should not regard this theology as a historic fact that is dead and gone. Since it is primarily a mode of thought, it cannot be considered as out of date, as something that has lost its value; today as much as ever, the school of Christ, such as the monastery is, bears witness to this fact.[140]

The monastery, the school of Christ, has only one essential purpose: to lead men back to God. In a very special way it is also a school of charity, where the study of this virtue is pursued, its problems discussed and solved, not so much by any mental process of reasoning as by experience and the very truth of things.[141] For Cistercians charity is the compendium of man's complete re-education.[142] The Abbot of Rievaulx resumed his monastic ideal in his *Mirror of Charity*, which, as St Bernard considered and had desired it to be, was a kind of spiritual directory for Cistercian monks. In fact it is a guide to the ways of divine love, for these monastic writers could not conceive a doctrine which was not at

135. See *supra*, p. xxxi.
136. Cf. Ph. Delhaye, "Un example de Théologie monastique au XIIᵉ siècle" in *Jumièges*, t. II, p. 786.
137. So Y. Congar remarks in his article *Théologie* in the *Dict. Théol. Cath.* XV, col. 345: this theology involves a certain impulse and grace which breaks out into praise of the goodness and glory of the God who is contemplated.
138. The opening words of the Prologue of the Rule of St Benedict.
139. *S. Benedicti Regula monachorum*, c. 2 and 63.
140. M. D. Chenu, "Culture et théologie à Jumièges après l'ère féodale" in *Jumièges*, t. II, p. 781.
141. William of Saint-Thierry, *De natura et dignitate amoris*, IX, 26; P.L. 184, col. 396d.
142. *Spec.* V, 8, 512c.

H

the same time a regulating of charity, a way to wisdom. To the man
who enters the school of Christ, Aelred clearly and emphatically
points out *the* way, the way of charity.[143]

The teaching of the school of Christ, which is knowledge joined
with love, supposes and demands the backing of asceticism. It is
incompatible with mediocrity of life. Love is the eye that will permit
us to see God,[144] and the sharpness of its vision is in proportion to
its purity. On this point Aelred is quoting Cassian:[145] "All holiness
consists in purity of heart. . . . Despising the world brings purity of
heart, since all impurity of heart comes of loving the world. Loving
the world makes the heart unclean; consequently, he who despises
the world unreservedly has a heart free from all uncleanness."[146]
Those monks who remain attached to the world belong in spirit to
the world, even though they dwell within the cloister; they do not
belong to the school of charity: "So those of us . . . whose affections
are fixed on the things of earth, who bestow our love on any
worldly object, must expect trouble; our backbiting, our worrying
and envying one another will continue."[147]

The ideal proposed by Christ in his school is an arduous one.
How many are capable of forsaking "all they are fond of, their
self-will, so as to follow Christ stripped like him"?[148] Aelred was
under no illusions but was very much a realist, and his experiences
as abbot taught him not to take his monks for angels. He describes
for us the cracks and seams of monastic life and is in no way
surprised at them. He is aware that he is dealing with men, who,
returned from a more or less distant and disturbed land of unlikeness, still retain cupidity within them. A deep-rooted, clinging
weed, this cupidity cannot be uprooted in a single day, nor
destroyed by a few outbursts of fervor. The evils it breeds in the
souls of monks are countless. Adroitly and with a touch of ironic
humor Aelred unmasks all the obstacles to the triumph of charity

143. *Spec.* III, 36, 613b–c.
145. *Collat.* I, 4; *Sources chrétiennes*, p. 81.
147. *S. Oner.* XVIII, 435a.

144. *Spec.* I, 1, 505b.
146. *S. Temp.* XVI, 301c.
148. *S. Oner.* XXVI, 472c.

in the school of Christ. Envy, for example, consumes everything in those addicted to it: the heart of the envious man no longer contains anything but "bitterness and blindness."[149] The proud man is tortured by self-will and the urge to domineer: "How he is crossed, tormented! Put to the blush, crushed, bothered, shaken, disturbed, his mortification is past bearing . . . he sighs, sweats, is tortured."[150] Pride is the monk's most formidable enemy because it prevents him from giving himself to the action of God, and stirs up in him the urge to murmur and criticize, which, to Aelred's mind as to St Benedict's,[151] appears as the worst evil of monastic life. Some complain of being put out of their accustomed routine in the matter of food or sleep . . .;[152] others would like to correct the abbot or the other officials of the monastery;[153] still others, hankering regretfully after Egypt, harass their superiors with requests for outings to the world, and, if they are refused, go away rueful and in ill temper, filling the cloisters with their grievances and bitter comments.[154]

These pen-pictures are not a conventional literary device nor the product of a mere flair for satire—though sometimes one gets that impression; rather they reveal Aelred's primary concern, which was to make Rievaulx a genuine school of Christ. For nearly twenty years he ruled his monastery and used all his endeavor to make it advance in this spirit. But it is good to emphasize that Aelred had a cordial welcome for all who came to Rievaulx seeking God. No one appealed to his goodness in vain,[155] and it was only very seldom that he could decide of his own accord to send someone back to the world.[156] To his mind, the monastery was not a gathering of select souls who came to find a favorable atmosphere for their full flowering, but a family of Christians who, united together in a charity which ripened into friendship, were striving to achieve their salvation. Everyone, weak as well as strong, should find at Rievaulx

149. *S. Ined.*, p. 72.   150. *Spec.* II, 26, 575a–b.
151. *S. Benedicti Regula monachorum*, c. 34, 40 and 41.
152. *S. Ined.*, p. 148.   153. *S. Temp.* XV, 296a.
154. *S. Ined.*, p. 149.   155. *Vita*, p. 39.   156. *Vita*, p. 40.

a haven of peace, the welcome and joyous and all-embracing peace of charity.[157]

A house as catholic as the Church, a world in miniature[158]—such was Rievaulx. The supreme glory to which it aspired was to be a Mother of Mercy. Fashioned after the abbot's own heart, it offered all God's wayfarers the shelter they longed for.[159]

157. *Vita.*, p. 37.
158. D. Knowles, *The Monastic Order* . . . , pp. 259 and 376.
159. *Vita*, p. 37.

CHAPTER 4

ERUDITIO AND DISCIPLINA

A MONK enters the school of Christ to seek God. There, instead of being left to his own initiative and consequently free to choose the details of his way of life—where too often self-will with all its caprices would insinuate itself—he submits voluntarily to formative disciplines.[1] Experience has proved how efficacious these are if one accepts them in the spirit in which they were devised. A considerable number of them could be enumerated but, after a study of Aelred's works, we prefer to reduce them to these three which are fundamental: Sacred Scripture together with the commentaries of the Fathers, the liturgy with its symbolic actions, and the Rule of St Benedict along with the Observances of

---

1. There is a delicate nuance of meaning between *eruditio* and *disciplina*. While the two terms are most often synonyms in patristic and medieval tradition (see the article by Dom Jean Leclercq: "Disciplina" in *Dict. Spir.*, col. 1294), the word *disciplina* quite frequently takes on a special significance with the Cistercians of the twelfth century: it designates the Cistercian observance (*ibid.*, col. 1298). The two terms are quite clearly distinguished in certain texts of Aelred; on the one hand, *eruditio* is *reformatio*, the restoration of wisdom in us (*S. Oner.* I, 363c); and Sacred Scripture is the source of this reformation in faith, hope and charity (*ibid.*). On the other hand, *disciplina ordinis* is repeatedly used by him to designate the *necessaria exercitia* of monastic formation. He speaks, for example, of a novice *traditus a reverendissimo abbate nostro meae parvitati disciplinis regularibus instituendus* (*Spec.* II, 17, 562a); and of another *quem ego regularibus disciplinis primus institui* (*Am.*, 698d, p. 188). Cf. C. Dumont, in *Collect. Ord. Cist. Ref.* 18 (1956) 177, n.1, for further references. With this distinction in mind, the reader will better understand the arrangement of this chapter: the first two sections dealing more with *eruditio* while the third deals with *disciplina*.

85

Cîteaux as interpreted by the Abbot of Rievaulx in the light of charity.

The personal influence of the abbot is, of course, a decisive factor in monastic formation, but we have already considered Aelred as the father and teacher of his monks in the preceding chapter, which seemed the natural place to consider it. The influence on a monk of the community spirit, which he is continually absorbing and which molds him, is also of vital importance, but we shall leave the study of this factor to a later chapter. Examined in relation to the concrete aspects of monastic formation, which, like all experience, is of a personal character, it will bring out better what a true Christian formation is, a formation in the Church that aims at the full development of the human person and his assimilation to God, who is one and triune, a personal Being whose life is friendship.

Source of Re-education: Sacred Scripture and the Fathers

The first thing that strikes us in reading the works of the medieval monks is their familiarity with the Bible.[2] These spiritual men, Aelred and St Bernard, William of Saint-Thierry, Richard of Saint-Victor and so many others, lived in a scriptural atmosphere, were saturated with the spirit of the Bible; their thoughts were molded by Scripture. At that period, of course, the Bible was the book *par excellence* of every Christian and at no stage of his intellectual development, from the rudiments of reading[3] to the *Sacra Pagina* of the Scholastics,[4] did he discard it; but there was a difference

---

2. J. Leclercq, *The Love of Learning and the Desire for God,* pp. 87–109. See also B. Smalley, *The Study of the Bible in the Middle Ages,* 2nd edition, Oxford, 1952. G. Spicq, *Esquisse d'une histoire de l'exégèse au Moyen Age,* Paris, 1944. M. Dumontier, *Saint Bernard et la Bible,* Bruges, 1953.

3. P. Riche, "Le Psautier, livre de lecture élémentaire" in *Actes du Congrès mérovingien de Poitiers,* 1952 (*Etudes mérovingiennes,* 1953).

4. G. Pare, A. Brunet, P. Tremblay, *La Renaissance du XIIe siècle . . .,* p. 307.

between the way Scripture was read in the schools and in the monasteries. In the latter, to read the Bible was to seek for God; in the former, the study of the sacred books tended to take the form of question and answer.[5] The monk's primary concern in reading the Word of God was not to satisfy his intellectual curiosity but to stimulate his quest for God: "Fervor, not questions, are your quest; incitement to charity, not subtlety of argument."[6] There was one text which they particularly cherished: "When all this happened to them, it was a symbol; the record of it was written as a warning to us" (I Cor 10:11).[7] This text, they felt, set the seal of approval on their preference for the allegorical interpretation of Scripture. Spiritual men have a kind of privilege to pry into the depths of God's message, and the Spirit favors them with a kind of charism to reveal these depths to others.

We shall never be attuned to these monastic writers if we have not grasped the deep-reaching significance of their familiarity with the Word of the living God. By a constant communion of mind and heart with the divine Presence, they attained a deeply religious understanding and an all-embracing view—rather like the *gnosis* of the Fathers—of man's problem and the divine plan of salvation. Their spiritual insight into Scripture discovered the sacred history of the human race and the individual soul's spiritual journey, and they recognized there the stages of the soul's ascent to God. The thoroughly religious atmosphere which we sense when we read them comes from this divine wellspring at which they unfailingly drank: "The test of the tree is in its fruit. The success of medieval exegesis is obviously due to the fact that the medieval exegetes read the Bible under the influence of the Spirit who inspired it. This explains why they could discover, as if by instinct, the true meaning of the text, for their minds were spontaneously in tune with the

5. M. D. Chenu, *Introduction à l'étude de Saint Thomas d'Aquin*, Paris, 1950, p. 72.

6. *Jesu*, P.L. 184, 856a.

7. *S. Temp.* VII, 247d. *S. Temp.* XXI, 333c. *S. Ined.*, pp. 42, 63 and 146.

thought of the sacred books. They lived the reality which their exegesis sought to discover behind the words."[8] Aelred himself will tell us what part the Scriptures played in his own monastic formation and in the teaching he imparted to his monks. According to the counsel of his holy father St Benedict, the Word of God was regarded by him as "the most unerring rule of human life."[9]

Ever since he entered the monastery, the reading of Sacred Scripture was a source of delight to him: "There and then I devoted myself to the study of Scripture; before that, blear-eyed worldling that I was, even a superficial reading had been impossible. As the sacred writings became ever more my delight, whatever the world had taught me seemed increasingly unimportant."[10] Jocelin of Furness, who wrote the *Life* of Waldef, has recorded for us Aelred's zeal in reading the Bible: "what efforts he made and how well he used that keen mind of his."[11] Very soon he came to realize that Sacred Scripture must in future become the ultimate criterion of his doctrine and the norm of his judgments. Any other testimony is acceptable only in so far as it is in accord with the divine Word,[12] and nothing can compare with the delight the soul experiences in meditating on the Bible. "Nothing that lacked the seasoning salt of Holy Scripture could fully captivate me."[13] Like St Bernard, whom William of Saint-Thierry described as "remarkably meditative," the abbot of Rievaulx had long pondered and relished the Holy Scriptures and his teaching was the fruit of his reflection. This familiarity of his with the Bible is well exemplified in the treatise *When Jesus Was Twelve*.

On becoming abbot, and consequently teacher of his monks, Aelred felt the urge to communicate to them the Word of God,

---

8. G. Spicq, *Esquisse d'une histoire de l'exégèse. . .* , p. 372.
9. *Regula monachorum*, c. 73, ed. McCann, p. 161.
10. *Am.*, Prolog., 659b, p. 2.
11. *Vita Waltheni* in *Acta Sanctorum*, Augusti, t. I, edit. Palme, 258c.
12. *Am.*, Prolog., 660a, p. 4; I, 662a, p. 10.
13. *Am.*, Prolog., 660a, p. 4.

"as in duty bound, yes, but particularly because I love you."[14] To accomplish this mission fittingly, he had the gift of a spiritual understanding of the Scriptures, which might be called an inspiration in the wide sense:[15] "Under your inspiration Isaiah wrote. Do you, in turn, inspire me, I pray, with understanding of his writings."[16] He realized, too, that he was God's interpreter to his monks: "It is all God's free gift, entrusted to me, intended for you."[17] But his authority and persuasive conviction were due also to his personal experience of the things of God. An abbot has to be a spiritual man, who, with the aid of divine light, has acquired a sense of the supernatural. There are certain things which only experience can teach: "Without tasting there is no telling."[18] And the man who speaks from experience (*ex sententia*)[19] will likewise know how to express it so as to make this experience something to be desired.

Aelred had reached such a degree of familiarity with Scripture that he constantly referred to it. The men and women of the Bible became his friends, and he automatically chose biblical incidents when he wanted to illustrate his theological teaching or even his psychological observations. In the second sermon *De Oneribus*, for example, each vision is explained by an event chosen from Scripture.[20] Similarly the various friendships he described in his treatise *On Spiritual Friendship* are illustrated by some figure in the sacred books. Even his historical works have their quota of scriptural references: the genealogy of the kings of England, for instance, is traced back to Adam; King Alfred was brought up on the psalms,[21] and related stories from the Bible to his companions;[22] Queen

14. *S. Oner.* I, 365b.
15. See G. Bardy, "L'inspiration des Pères de l'Eglise" in *Rech. Sc. Rel.* 40 (1952) 7–26. 16. *S. Oner.* I, 365d. 17. *S. Oner.* I, 365c. 18. *S. Ined.*, p. 106.
19. *Ibid.* In his article on contemplation in the *Dict. Spir.*, col. 1954, Dom J. Déchanet translates St Bernard's phrase *ex sententia* (P.L. 183, 794a) as "to repeat according to one's desire", which does not seem to be a correct translation, since *ex sententia* (*sensus, sentire*) means here simply "by experience."
20. *S. Oner.* II, 368–369. 21. *Geneal. Reg. Angl.*, 718d.
22. *Ibid.*, 721.

Matilda is another Esther,[23] and King Edward appears as a just man of Israel.[24]

But Aelred's chief interest does not lie there. Called to guide souls, he, who was himself a lover of Holy Scripture, encouraged his monks to taste for themselves the divine savor of the inspired Word. In a monastery, assiduous reading of the Bible is a necessity: "You, dearest brethren, have taken leave of secular business, of the world's cares and anxieties, and so, unencumbered, entered the lists against impure spirits and your own selfishness; for you, consequently, the study of the Scriptures is especially urgent and necessary."[25] They must do all in their power to return to their sacred reading with freshness of mind and avoid the boredom that results from the monotonous repetition of the same exercise.[26] They can never leave aside their reflection which supplies their intellect with a norm for gauging their own spiritual experiences[27] and the value of the sayings of the ancients.[28] This is true to such an extent that he who has not the authority of Scripture behind him is a fool: "It is sheer madness, in my opinion, to doubt that the more a man's life conforms to the teaching of Scripture the better he is."[29]

A monk must approach Scripture with a keen sense of its sacredness. The Bible is full of mysteries and secrets, and in proportion as one's spiritual awareness is purified, God reveals its unsuspected depths, "when he discovers to us partially and yet intimately the limitless ocean of his mysteries."[30] By means of vivid and realistic expressions drawn from the Bible, Aelred endeavors to help us get a glimpse of the hidden riches of the Bible in the plan of the divine economy. Scripture may aptly be called God's womb for it bears within it the thoughts of God.[31] A man who acquires an

---

23. *Ibid.*, 736b.
24. *Vita Ed.*, 747a–b (the King's prayer), 774c (account of his death).
25. *S. Oner.* I, 364b.
26. *Ibid.*, 364c.
27. *Spec.*, II, 14, 558b–c; *S. Ined.*, p. 143.
28. *Am.*, I, 662a, p. 11.
29. *Spec.* II, 17, 564c.
30. *S. Oner.* XI, 405c.
31. *S. Oner.* XXXI, 496c.

understanding of revelation, judges all things according to the heart of God: "By heart of God is meant understanding the secrets of Holy Scripture."[32] Following the Fathers, these medieval writers, convinced that the Scriptures were full of hidden mysteries,[33] never tired of pondering the sacred text in all its aspects, not indeed with the precision of modern exegetes, but certainly with a fervor that equalled this precision. "We should not be surprised at the great variety of possible interpretations. God who is Spirit surpasses the limitations of our human words. He would teach us more than one lesson. The abundance of his message cannot be confined within the narrow limits of our language."[34]

Everything in Scripture has been ordered according to the plan of the Holy Spirit, its unfathomable depths and its application to the needs of each individual. It was he who inspired Scripture and imparted to it its richness—"there is no end to its meaning"[35]—and it is he, too, who adapts it to each soul's capacity.[36] His use of it is an art all his own: to one, he reveals this truth; to another, he communicates that insight. Under his inspiration the Word of God appears ever new.[37] The amazing wheel Ezechiel saw in his vision is a symbol of Sacred Scripture. It can be seen by us in any of its four aspects—that is, its four senses, adapted to the needs of different souls: "its first side is for the literal sense, its second for the spiritual, its third for the allegorical, its fourth for the anagogical (i.e. the eschatological) meaning."[38]

When a man studies this living richness, he feels the need of recollection. The Word of God cannot be understood and relished except in a spirit of prayer: the spiritual fruit of holy reading (*lectio divina*) is a gift from the Spirit. Either at the beginning or the end of his sermons Aelred frequently invites his monks to pray.[39] Prayer

---

32. *S. Oner.* XXV, 467b.   33. *Ibid.*
34. G. Dumeige, *Richard de Saint-Victor et l'idée chrétienne de l'amour*, p. 24.
35. *S. Oner.* I, 363c–364a.   36. *S. Oner.* XIX, 438d.
37. *S. Oner.* I, 364a.   38. *S. Temp.* X, 264c-d.
39. *S. Temp.* XXI, 336a; *S. Oner.* III, 337a; IV, 380d; XX, 444c.

(oratio) is at once the condition for receiving the Word of God and the normal conclusion of reflection (meditatio) on the Holy Books.[40] A kind of reciprocal causality exists between these spiritual exercises. The abbot explains Sacred Scripture to his monks, that is sermo; he urges them to make direct contact with the Bible for themselves, that is lectio; and the fruit of this exercise is prayer, oratio.[41]

If a monk thus grows, by prayer and humility of heart, in the knowledge of the Scriptures, he will experience that spiritual understanding which is inevitably the mark and effect of a true conversion of soul, the passing from the darkness of Egypt to the light of Christ, who is the key to the Scriptures. From then on he will no longer be satisfied with the letter of the text but will seek its spirit[42] and will experience how replete the Word of God is with hidden treasure, "a wealth of holy secrets."[43] The medieval monastic writers were constantly seeking for the hidden meaning of Scripture, not that they despised the literal meaning—indeed they considered this the foundation of all other meanings—but, as spiritual men, they desired profit for their spiritual life.[44] They knew what they wanted: to come to a knowledge of the mysteries hidden beneath the veil of the letter.[45] A delicate task, because any real success in it can come only as a gift of God.

Like the perfect wife in the Book of Proverbs, the soul can, and indeed must, use all its own resources, but in the last analysis spiritual knowledge, wisdom and understanding are divine gifts, not human acquisitions—"all these the soul is given by her husband."[46] For the understanding of Scripture there must first of all be a purification of soul; a man can grasp God's mind only by becoming like to him. Study of Scripture, if it is to be spiritual, requires a reformation of life: "So, stripped of vice and clothed in virtue, let

40. S. Oner. IV, 380d.   41. S. Oner. III, 377a.
42. S. Oner. III, 376a; S. Ined., pp. 44, 45 and 48.
43. S. Temp. XVIII, 312b.   44. S. Temp. XXI, 327a-b.
45. S. Oner. XXVII, 479b; S. Ined., p. 48; Jesu, P.L. 184, 854a.
46. S. Temp. XXV, 356d.

him pass to the study of the Scriptures, that reformation of life go hand in hand with illuminations of mind."[47] The soul in this quest is to remain always humble and retain its sense of mystery: it is journeying through "a very forest of allegory." The Lord is there, to be sure, but hidden behind a veil of obscurity.[48] For all his application and keen desire, the spiritual man cannot fathom everything; when confronted with a very obscure text,[49] he acknowledges his inability to understand it. Only the proud in their blindness dare boast of their clear-sightedness and claim "there are no difficulties in Scripture."[50] Only they may indulge in any fanciful interpretation of the Bible; the religious man, on the contrary, has a deep reverence for the Word of God and is ever concerned for what becomes its sacredness.[51] However, the man with spiritual understanding is still free and can at times permit himself considerable latitude in his interpretations: in the series of sermons *De Oneribus*, for example, the Medes successively stand for the heralds of Antichrist, the Apostles of the last days, and finally—*mutatio in melius*—the good angels.[52] Modern exegetes would be somewhat skeptical of such a method, but it was quite legitimate in the Middle Ages.

The liberties these medieval monks appeared to take with the inspired text should not prevent us from understanding and admiring their enthusiastic attitude towards the Bible. Their example is a perennial lesson to us. In the Sacred Scriptures they were looking for God and they found him: "Everyone knows that the Lord Jesus is to be sought for in the Scriptures."[53] Every word of Scripture speaks of Christ, but only a soul that receives light from above can find him there. He lies hidden,[54] sometimes in deep mystery, in word-riddle and historical parable.[55] Of a sudden, at

---

47. *S. Oner.* XXVIII, 484d.   48. *S. Oner.* XXVII, 478a.
49. *S. Oner.* XXV, 471b.   50. *S. Oner.* XXX, 491b.
51. *S. Oner.* III, 374b and 375d; IV, 378a-b; V, 381a; IX, 400a; XI, 406b-d.
52. *S. Oner.* IV, 379c-d; XI, 408b; XII, 409b and 412a.
53. *S. Oner.* XXVII, 478a.   54. *S. Temp.* XI, 276c.
55. *S. Oner.* XXVII, 478a. Cf. H. de Lubac, *Exégèse médiévale*, Ière partie, p. 486, Coll. *Théologie* 41, Aubier, Paris, 1959.

a time of his own choosing, he reveals himself to the soul that waits for him and desires him. It is carried away in wonder when it sees him emerging from the dense forest of allegory.[56] At such moments it understands better the rich complexity of God's Word and admires the great mystery contained in the Bible.[57] It experiences the mystery of Christ through the understanding of the Scriptures: "Who would know Christ, the Power of God, must study to understand Scripture."[58]

In monastic theology, *lectio divina* is not simply an intellectual exercise, but a communing with the living God who reveals himself to us through his Word. It is the occasion of a visit from the Lord,[59] "a reading with God, in his company, with his help, a reading that involves two."[60] This spiritual exercise is accompanied by a relish which, surpassing a mere notional knowledge, leads to a true religious experience suited to each individual. This light which comes from the inspired text or—it is important to note—on the occasion of the *lectio*, is received by the soul as a personal message, which is meant for it and serves to "build up its faith."[61] The following quotation, which illustrates this point, shows at the same time the difference between the attitude of the modern scientific exegete towards the Bible, when he is no more than a scientific expert, and the medieval monk's intense awareness that he is in contact with Someone: "Whatever is fittingly suggested by these holy pages, to rouse faith, strengthen hope, set charity aflame, be sure the Holy Spirit has both hidden it there and discovered it to you."[62] The monk of the Middle Ages was not primarily interested in the letter of the text, as is the exegete of today, but in the profit

56. *Ibid.*   57. *S. Temp.* XI, 276c.
58. *S. Temp.* XXIV, 350c.
59. *S. Temp.* XVIII, 309a and XXII, 399a.
60. M. Dumontier, *Saint Bernard et la Bible,* p. 50.
61. *S. Ined.,* p. 92; *S. Oner.* I, 365b, favorite themes of St Gregory (P.L. 76, 1302a) and of St Bernard (P.L. 183, 859a and 986c-d).
62. *S. Oner.* I, 364a.

he could draw from it for his spiritual life. The purpose of the *lectio* was to stimulate devotion.[63]

Aelred knew the classical methods of traditional exegesis: the investigation of the four senses,[64] the reminiscences suggested by the mere similarity of words, association of names and images, poetical evocations, etc. Texts of Scripture were often sought to support a preconceived spiritual synthesis to which they fitted. The reader never gets the impression that these are the product of the imagination of some excitable mystic, but the work of a soul whose deep faith calls for purity of life and whose desire to live in accordance with the Word of God is evident. There is a constant tendency in Aelred's sermons to apply Scripture to his own life and the lives of his monks. Instead of allegorical flights, medieval monks seemed to prefer the tropological exposition which looked to "the development of virtue."[65] "It is usually more interesting and useful,"[66] as Aelred remarks. Incarnate Wisdom did, in fact, make Scripture a powerful means for reforming our lives; nothing can resist the Word of God: "The sword of the spirit, God's Word cuts through, makes an end of all that opposes it."[67] This Word has been transmitted to us by God's friends and prophets for the purpose of helping us return to God, since the Lord makes it a means of restoration, "the very fount of all our re-education."[68] Become part of our lives, it will prevent us from forgetting God and help to re-make in us the image, absorbed in the thought of God: "The memory is restored by the teaching of Holy Scripture."[69]

Primarily a source of doctrine, Scripture is also for Aelred a divine norm for the guidance of souls. Nothing can gainsay the authority of the Word of God; nothing can escape it.[70] A principle

---

63. *S. Ined.*, p. 130. Cf. *Jesu*, P.L. 184, 856a.

64. *S. Temp.* X, 265. In this sermon (under the title "in ramis palmarum" though it is actually a sermon *De Adventu*) Aelred examines the four senses of Scripture, explains each of them and "tries" them in turn.

65. *S. Oner.* XXVI, 471c; XXVIII, 481a.   66. *S. Temp.* XXV, 353b.

67. *S. Ined.*, p. 97. Cf. Eph 6:17.   68. *S. Oner.* I, 363c.

69. *Spec.* I, 5, 509b.   70. *S. Ined.*, p. 143.

of restoration, it will guide us on the way of return and "re-inform" us by wisdom.[71] A monk who has tasted God in *lectio divina* knows that the sacred text puts him in contact with the Lord, and is convinced that "every line, every word has been written for each one of us."[72] The soul that is enlightened by the Holy Spirit reads in the narrative of sacred history the vicissitudes of its own journeying; it understands better God's action in sanctifying it. Holy Scripture is the occasion of spiritual experiences whence the soul draws light, healing and consolation.[73]

To Aelred's way of thinking, the primary means of monastic education is, therefore, contact, almost continual contact, with the Holy Scriptures seen as the Word of the living God. The text of the Bible is light to our darkness,[74] and our spiritual mirror.[75] The allegories he discovers and studies in his *meditatio* are for him not mere literary adornments, but respond to his inmost desire to fathom ever deeper the mysteries of God, and are devised for "the building-up of faith."[76] To his assiduous familiarity with Scripture he owes that vision of the plan of salvation which gives to his works their unity and their deeply religious tone. His sense of history comes to him from revelation: "For in God's Word we are reminded of the past, we see into the present, we foresee the future."[77] God's plan is apparent to him in the continuity of the Old and New Testaments.[78] The Old is entirely prophetical and finds its fulfillment in Christ and the Church. The Gospels and the prophecies are seen together, one in the other, "as a wheel within a wheel."[79]

Let us remark here how topical is such a concept of Scripture as an essential source of doctrine. In the principal fields of religious culture today one becomes aware of a desire for a more intimate

71. *S. Oner.* I, 363c.   72. M. Dumontier, *Saint Bernard et la Bible,* p. 170.
73. *S. Oner.* XXVI, 476b-d.
74. *S. Ined.,* p. 31.   75. *Spec.* II, 14, 559c; *Inst.,* 20, p. 193.
76. *S. Ined.,* p. 92.   77. *S. Ined.,* p. 31.   78. *S. Temp.* III, 230b.
79. *Ibid.,* 230c.

contact, a more personal and living study, a more real familiarity with the sacred text of revelation. Contemporary exegesis is rediscovering the deep-reaching meaning of the spiritual understanding of the Scriptures. The Second Vatican Council has expressed the desire that theology should be sustained more by the Bible. Pastoral efforts are being directed towards leading the people back to the liturgical life, in which the Word of God is proclaimed daily by the Church. A renewal of the methods of catechetical instruction aims at establishing Christian education on the inspired books as its basis.[80] The meaning of history, which is rightly esteemed today, is leading men to see the economy of salvation, with all its work of preparation, its decisive moments and its eschatological tension, as God's intervention in time.[81]

For the monks of the Middle Ages, the constant reading of Scripture was inseparably linked with the reading of the Fathers who had written commentaries on it. This familiar contact with the writings of the Fathers made monastic theology a continuation of the spirituality of the early centuries and stamped it with a veritable cult for tradition, the guarantee of doctrinal purity. At Rievaulx every monk who had the least smattering of learning was accustomed to read Augustine, Gregory, Ambrose, *et al.*, at least in some of their better-known and more easily accessible manuscripts. Hence Aelred, commenting on the Scriptures in chapter, had attentive hearers. This initial acquaintance of some of his listeners with the Fathers allowed him to choose for his comments the texts most suitable to his large and heterogeneous community: "Those of you whose reading of the commentaries of the holy Fathers is habitual have no need of much else on this subject; and the Brothers, I am sure, will have no objection to listening to

80. Cf. P. Hitz, "Théologie et catéchèse" in *Nouv. Rev. Théol.* 77 (1955) 910; also C. Davis, *The Study of Theology* (1962), ch. 4: "The Theology of Preaching", pp. 48–70.

81. See M. Flick and Z. Alszeghy, "Theologia della Storia" in *Gregorianum* 35 (1954) 256–98.

something different."[82] With regard to the former, however, the Abbot was exacting: he expected them to have direct and personal contact with the sacred text so as to live by it and find God in it, instead of just endlessly reading the commentaries: "It is more than enough for such as are sunk in the busy doings of this world or entangled in the meshes of unavoidable duty . . . that they become acquainted with commentaries on Scripture . . . but you, dear friends . . . have more than a reason . . . you have the duty of studying the Scriptures themselves."[83]

Aelred had too great a love for his holy father St Benedict, "who fully shared the spirit of all the saints,"[84] not to comply with his exhortation to all his monks to become students of "the holy Fathers of the Catholic Church" so as to attain to God "by the straight road."[85] Besides, his Cistercian training was bound to have imbued him with that devoted esteem for the Fathers that is extolled by the *Little Exordium*, with perhaps calculated insistence, in the words "they were the spokesmen of the Holy Spirit, whose ordinances it were sacrilegious to neglect."[86] Aelred belonged very much to the monasticism of the Middle Ages, which inherited the spirituality of the Fathers. From them he learned to take an all-embracing view of the history of salvation and the mysteries of Christianity with their inter-connection and harmony, a kind of synthesis that reminds us of the *Gnosis* of the Fathers and sheds light on the liturgical and ascetical development of the teaching of the Abbot of Rievaulx. Like St Bernard and others, he added to it the more subjective and personal element, the element of experience, which will be studied in Part 3. Akin to the Fathers in their manner of thinking, the monks of the Middle Ages yet differed from them

---

82. *S. Temp.* XIII, 285a.   83. *S. Oner.* I, 364b.

84. *S. Temp.* VII, 248a. Aelred writes: *ut quidam ait.* This *quidam* is St Gregory the Great; see *Dialogues*, book 2, ch. 8, P.L. 66, 150b.

85. *Rule of St Benedict*, ch. 73, *op. cit.*, p. 99.

86. *Exordium Cisterciensis Cenobii*, c. XV: Ph. Guignard, *Les monuments primitifs de la règle cistercienne*, Dijon, 1878, p. 72.

in that they did not belong to the fourth century, had not the same function in the Church and were animated by a new outlook.

Many passages in Aelred's works prove that he was at pains to refer constantly to the writings and the ideas of the Fathers, and that he instilled a like respect for tradition in his monks. When he had to "christianize" Cicero's treatise on friendship he had recourse to the most authentic sources: "Time and again I gave the matter thought in my efforts to base myself on Scripture. In the holy Fathers I found much on friendship."[87] When he wished to give his sister guidance in her vocation as a recluse, he turned especially to the counsels of the Fathers; he went through their writings to compose a florilegium, "taking a detail here and there . . . from the teachings of the Fathers."[88] The orthodoxy of his teaching is thus assured by the authority of the Fathers.

Similarly in the arrangements of the liturgy he perceives, or supposes, that there is a governing plan which shows forth the wisdom of the Fathers. For example, why is the account of the entry of Jesus into Jerusalem read during Advent? "The holy Fathers, it seems to me, had good reason in so decreeing."[89] The most significant reference—a rather curious one it is true—is when Aelred appeals to the authority of the Fathers against all innovations, even in the matter of sacred music. We shall quote it at length for it reveals his whole mentality: "So it comes about that what the Fathers instituted as a means of helping the less fervent to devotion is made to provide unbecoming amusement. No, the texts are not to be made subservient to the tunes; music is to be allowed only when by bringing out the meaning of the words, it helps to devotion. [Here the authority of St Augustine is quoted.] In fact, however, the restrictions imposed by the Fathers are considered lacking in refinement and condemned as such; the rules of chant which the Holy Spirit, with the blessed Fathers Augustine,

87. *Am.,* Prolog., 660a, p. 4.   88. *Inst.* I, p. 177.
89. *S. Temp.* X, 264c.

Ambrose and particularly Gregory for his spokesmen, dictated, are set aside and in their place we are given so-called iberian lullabies and heaven knows what senseless trumpery provided by some schoolman or other."[90]

Which of the Fathers had the greatest influence on Aelred's doctrinal formation? It is beyond doubt—we have his own word for it—that he always preferred St Augustine. He never parted with the *Confessions;* this book had guided and encouraged him in his own conversion, and it remained the companion of his later years: "Augustine's *Confessions* hardly ever left his hands."[91] A study of Aelred's works reveals countless quotations from, or allusions to, the doctrine of St Augustine: the first chapters of the *Mirror of Charity* could be annotated with innumerable references to Augustine's works.[92] As for his treatise *On the Soul* the reader has only to consult the *Index auctorum* compiled by C. H. Talbot to be persuaded of the chief source of Aelred's anthropology. And yet from "wholly Augustinian principles . . . a very personal system of thought was to develop."[93] The Abbot of Rievaulx was a man of clear-sight and a thinker; he re-thought and pondered for a long time the doctrine he had imbibed in his reading and, in the light of his personal experience, composed a synthesis of it that bore the mark of his own genius.

Next to St Augustine, though certainly not to the same degree, Aelred was influenced by St Gregory[94] and St Ambrose.[95] How

---

90. *Spec.* II, 23, 571d and 572b (Dubois translation).   91. *Vita,* p. 50.

92. P. Courcelle gives a persuasive example of this in the *Revue des Etudes augustiniennes* 111-12 (1957) 163–74.

93. L. Bouyer, *The Cistercian Heritage,* p. 134.

94. Cf. *S. Oner.* X, 403b; *S. Oner.* XVII, 433a; *Spec.* II, 572b; *S. Temp.* VII, 248a (See *supra,* n. 83). Aelred's very noticeable fondness for the moral application of Scripture is an indication of St Gregory's influence, which was very marked in the Middle Ages.

95. See P.L. 195, 403b; 479c; 572b; 683d; 688d; 694a; 695d. Cf. E. Gilson, *The Mystical Theology of St Bernard,* p. 70: "It is unneccessary then to say that St Ambrose should be regarded as one important source of the Cistercian mysticism."

much did he owe to Origen? It is more difficult to discover traces
of the Greek Fathers in Aelred than in St Bernard. The catalogue
of the library of Rievaulx informs us that Origen's works were
within his reach. If we recall the vogue the celebrated Alexandrian
enjoyed at Clairvaux, it is possible to admit that Aelred, too, was
familiar with his works. Fr Bouyer has noted in Aelred "a view of
the Biblical mysteries and of their application to the Church and to
the life of the individual Christian in Christ which betrays the
influence of Origen too clearly to leave any doubt that Aelred had
himself drawn from that source."[96]

Aelred liked to present to his monks the Fathers he admired.
Sometimes he recalled the example of their conversion to God;
skilled in the wisdom of the world, they knew how to become wise
in divine things:[97] "Cyprian . . . Ambrose . . . Augustine and
Jerome what did they, but put all that the world had taught them
at the service of the Church, to her defense and advantage?" At
other times he lauded their great learning which made them shine
like the sun in the firmament of the Church.[98] In spite of his great
esteem for them, however, Aelred did not feel obliged to embrace
all their interpretations or accept all their opinions.[99] He was their
disciple and admirer, but he retained his individuality.

The Liturgy

To gain a clear idea of the importance of the liturgical life in a
monk's spiritual formation, it is enough to examine some sermons
for Advent, the Annunciation, Easter or Pentecost,[100] in which

---

96. L. Bouyer, *The Cistercian Heritage*, p. 132. On the influence of Origen,
see for example Anselme Hoste, *Quand Jésus eut douze ans* (*Sources chrétiennes:
Textes monastiques d'Occident*, Paris, 1958).   97. *S. Oner.* XXVII, 479c.
98. *S. Oner.* X, 403b.   99. See for example *S. Oner.* XVII, 433a-b.
100. *De Adventu Domini, S. Temp.* I, 209–20 and *S. Ined*, pp. 31–37. *De
Assumptione Sanctae Marie, S. Ined.*, pp. 161–75. *In die Pentecosten, S. Ined.*,
pp. 106–12. *In die Paschae, S. Ined.*, pp. 94–100.

Aelred recalls the outstanding phases of the history of salvation and draws apt and practical applications from them to the journey of the individual soul. And we shall better understand then how closely inter-connected are the reading of Sacred Scripture, the preaching in chapter and the celebration of the liturgy in the monastery. These three elements form part of one living unity. Coming from the church to the cloister, the monks of the Middle Ages were nourished by the same Word of God. They recognized that what had been foretold in Scripture was fulfilled before their eyes in the liturgical mysteries.[101]

According to Aelred, God has two principal means, both of a mysterious efficacy, for bringing the divine economy of salvation to us and accomplishing it in us. We are reminded of God's will and salvific blessings, what today would be called the *kerygma*, by the text of the Scriptures and by the action of the liturgy: "Jesus, our Lord and Savior . . . has, in his care of us, given us not merely the record in the Scriptures of his saving deeds, but re-presented them for us through symbolic actions."[102] What is proclaimed by the divine Word is re-presented by a sacred action. Scripture and liturgy, wedded ever together, lead us to contemplate the history of our salvation in order that we may share personally in it. The work of redemption is thus constantly present to the minds of these monks, not as a mere subject for meditation but as something to which they are totally committed. The feast of the Annunciation, for example, is for them a day of great joy: "Blessed day, hour, time;"[103] it heralds their liberation, the beginning of their return to God: "that holy day, the source and cause of all holy days,"[104] "all the liberty and hope that is ours . . . began today."[105] Thus they live over again the events which brought them joy when they read

---

101. *S. Oner.* XVI, 427a.

102. *S. Temp.* VIII, 251b. We find reference in this passage to the threefold liturgical *sacramentum*—past, present and future—of which St Thomas was to speak so distinctly later.　　103. *S. Ined.*, p. 89.

104. *S. Ined.*, p. 77.　　　　　　　105. *S. Temp.* VIII, 251c.

of them in their *lectio divina*. As God's Word in Holy Scripture reveals to them the meaning of history in the mind of God—"In the Word of God we are reminded of the past, see into the present, foresee the future"[106]—so the celebration of the liturgy speaks to them of their redemption, of hope and beatitude, which are the three phases of the mystery of Christ: "We see what Christ suffered on our behalf; what, even at present, he bestows on us; what he has waiting for us in the life to come."[107]

These symbolic actions, these liturgical re-presentations, require in a monk the same openness of mind, the same humble, yearning attention with which he approaches *lectio divina*, where God communicates himself to him. God reveals to us by symbols what the concepts and words themselves are incapable of expressing: "Words of ours could not express the might and sweetness of that anointing . . .; what man's word cannot convey, God makes known—through symbolic actions."[108]

The liturgy uses words, vestments and symbolic gestures for its expression and if we are to grasp the hidden meaning of these sacred actions, we have need to acquire, with the help of divine grace, spiritual understanding. The hymns and chant and lights are not ends in themselves; moreover extravagance in these external means is unbecoming a genuinely religious soul. Here we detect the note of primitive Cîteaux, traceable to St Stephen Harding or more immediately to St Bernard. The saints, whose praise is Christ, are not glorified by mere earthly symbols; these are an invitation to rise to the hidden reality signified in the liturgy and it is then that the action takes on its full meaning, "because of its symbolism."[109]

---

106. *S. Ined.*, p.31.   107. *S. Temp.* XXIII, 340b-c.

108. *S. Temp.* III, 227d. The *res* here are the events commemorated in the Epiphany liturgy.

109. *S. Temp.* XXII, 336c-d. According to Aelred, the significance of these liturgical symbols is as follows: "Chant signifies the saints' constant celebration because of the unspeakable joy they have in God. Hymns signify that unutterable praise by which they always praise God. . . . Lights signify that perpetual light in which the saints of God dwell."

Like the frequent reading of Scripture, the celebration of the liturgy directs us towards the mystery of God. As the inspired text contains a hidden meaning which stimulates the spiritual man to seek it and which, when discovered, is a salutary experience, so each feast and each liturgical season has its "sacrament" which stimulates the soul's attention and fervor.[110]

The action of the liturgy is, in fact, the expression of the central mystery of the plan of redemption, the mystery of Christ,[111] which should never be far from the mind of a Christian, because such remembrance is a salutary grace.[112] At these moments of participation in the plan of salvation, it is the Lord who is present: "These many saints' feastdays, what are they but so many visits the Lord makes us for our encouragement?"[113]

In his sermons Aelred frequently reminds his monks of the sanctifying power of the solemnities that are the landmarks of the liturgical year and plot the course of their spiritual life. Each feast should stir up their fervor.[114] The desire of God should be renewed in their hearts by this re-presentation of the mysteries of salvation.[115]

The liturgical life, understood in this way, seemed to realize for Aelred the ideal he had formed of the monastery as "a house of God and gate of Heaven." In it is raised the mysterious ladder Jacob saw in his sleep, on which the angels were going up and coming down in their service of God and men.[116] All religious life must be a life in the Church, and even the hermit, "who devotes himself to possessing and not to bestowing God's gifts," can "gather the whole world to his loving heart," and "no other alms is more welcome to God, suited to his profession, profitable to men than this."[117] Without being selfishly unmindful of his fellow-men, a monk has to be totally devoted to the things of eternity. Even on earth, his life must, in some way, be a foreshadowing of the

110. *S. Temp.* X, 265a.
112. *S. Temp.* XXIII, 340b.
114. *S. Temp.* V, 238d.
116. *Vita Ed.*, 753b.

111. See *supra*, pp. 18-22.
113. *Ibid.*, 340a.
115. *S. Temp.* XXI, 326c.
117. *Inst.*, 28, p. 199.

"angelic life" of vision and praise that will be his occupation in heaven. On the feast of the Ascension the abbot reminds his monks that they are, as far as their weakness allows, to unite themselves with the liturgy of the angels, and follow the Lord on high by devotion and love.[118]

Everything in this monastic formation contributes to lead the monk to God, "to moving hearts . . . to fervor": the reading of Scripture, which proclaims God's plan of salvation, the celebration of the liturgy, which re-presents the principal mysteries of Christ and makes us share in them, and the conferences of the abbot. So Aelred could say to his community that monks lack nothing they need to set their hearts aflame with the love of God.[119]

Saint Benedict—Rule and Observances

"I think it in order, since we go by the name of monks, that we look closely into the binding force of our Rule; and since, to be sure, it contains much that refers to the interior life and much that deals with external observances, our chief quest must be to discover what we are most bound to by our Rule and our vows."[120] From his entry into religious life Aelred was at pains to grasp the essential meaning of the monastic life, and he showed a very high regard for, and a strong devotion to, St Benedict who passed on to us the spirit and wisdom of the Fathers: "In his Rule there glows the gold of most blessed Augustine, the silver of Jerome, the twice-dyed scarlet of Gregory, the jewel-like sayings of the holy Fathers; all of which goes to the adorning of this heavenly fabric."[121]

The spiritual exercises he prescribes, namely reading, prayer and meditation, are constantly associated with the assiduous reading of

---

118. *S. Ined.*, p. 100.   119. *S. Temp.* IX, 258d.
120. *Spec.* III, 35, 608b. In the letter to his sister, Aelred also takes his stand on the Rule of St Benedict, cf. *Inst.* 9, ed. Talbot, p. 184.
121. *S. Temp.* VII, 248a.

Scripture and the liturgical life, of which we have already spoken.[122] The external practices he imposes constituted the monastic observances which were especially dear to the Cistercians of the twelfth century, and which found in Aelred a stout defender.

St Benedict holds a fundamental place in the teaching of the Abbot of Rievaulx, in the sense—a sense incidentally that is expressive of Aelred's mentality—that the Father of monks has a role to fulfill in the Christian economy in relation to his disciples. Aelred, with his sense of Scripture, sees St Benedict as our Moses,[123] and his Rule, our Law, as the guidebook of our journey through the desert: "St Benedict has promulgated a law to us; we have only to keep true to it, he assures us, to become heirs of the kingdom of heaven. This law, my brethren, is his Rule."[124] There lies the chief interest of these few lines devoted to the study of St Benedict in Aelred's works. If we see him thus as the father, guide and model of monks, we shall better realize why Aelred regarded Sacred Scripture as the textbook of monastic formation and why he traced St Benedict's spirituality, and even the form of his expression, back to the Bible as its source.

As Moses was the instrument God used to liberate and instruct his Chosen People, so St Benedict is God's minister to bring monks back to himself:[125] "To us who live in darkness and death's shadow, God has sent a Moses—our Father St Benedict—to lead us, by his teaching, his Rule and his prayers, out from the Egypt of worldly living, on the strenuous road of virtuous living, to the contemplation of heavenly things."[126]

In regard to his monks, then, St Benedict fulfills the office of spiritual father and mediator. "He has begotten us in Christ Jesus,

122. On this whole question of the *spiritualia-corporalia* see C. Dumont, "L'Equilibre humain de la vie cistercienne, d'après le Bienheureux Aelred de Rievaulx" in *Collectanea O.C.R.* 18 (1956) 177–89.

123. See *supra*, pp. 17–28.   124. *S. Temp.* V, 240b.

125. This theme recurs repeatedly in his sermons; cf. *In festo S. Benedicti, S. Temp.* V, 238–45; VI, 245–47; VII, 247–51; *S. Ined.*, pp. 62–70, 71–76.

126. *S. Ined.*, p. 63.

through the Gospel."[127] Through him, monastic conversion, seen as a new birth, opens up a new life totally directed towards God.[128] God has willed that all the graces monks receive during their entire religious life should come to them through the mediation of their holy Father; growth in virtue, the spirit of compunction, the manna of spiritual consolation, etc., all come to them through his ministry:[129] "Your progress, such as it has been, in meditating, praying, compunction, devotion and so forth, has it not all been due to God's grace and come through the ministry and example of this Saint?"[130] St Benedict teaches us a necessary lesson, one that has lost none of its appropriateness today. While Moses made the actual journey with those who came out of Egypt and was physically present with them on their way to the Promised Land, St Benedict is no longer with his monks, who are wayfaring. He has left this earth, he has reached journey's end and this is precisely why he is their model in the great enterprise of salvation: "He has, to be sure, gone away from where we still are; he has reached a place to which, as yet, we have not come. . . . He has passed from earth to heaven, prison to palace, death to life, misery to glory."[131]

The one thing necessary is to make this passing (*transitus*) safely; St Benedict, our model, teaches us this essential lesson: "Even while he lived here in the body, in thought and desire he was already in heaven."[132] Moreover he found the "straight way" that leads back to God: "Christ was the way he took. . . . Through him he reached him."[133] A sure way, indeed, for it is the narrow way that "leads to life," while the broad and easy way of sinners "will end in hell and everlasting death."[134] As a young monk St Benedict learned by

127. *S. Temp.* V, 239a. *S. Temp.* VI, 245a.

128. This is a common feature of the doctrine of the Cistercians of the twelfth century; cf. A. Le Bail, "La paternité de Saint Benoît sur l'Ordre de Cîteaux" in *Collectanea O.C.R.* 9 (1947) 120–21.

129. *S. Temp.* V, 240b.

130. *Ibid.*, 239a.   131. *S. Temp.* VI, 245a-b.

132. *Ibid.*, 245b.   133. *Ibid.*

134. *Ibid.*, 246a.

experience how arduous is the path that leads to the heights: "Did he give up on that account? No, he kept on, and manfully persevered. First he practiced, later he taught. How otherwise could he teach us to follow him?"[135] In this way he merited to become what several Cistercians[136] have called the *form* of the monastic life, the type fashioned by God and proposed to monks who, striving to resemble him, may aim at the perfection of their state. If they choose him as guide and model, his disciples will "certainly reach the place this great saint has come to."[137] It will have to be admitted that one could hardly be more explicit about the meaning of the monastic life and the fatherhood of St Benedict in relation to those who serve under his Rule.

Cistercian Observances

The question of monastic observances held a special interest for the first Cistercians, an interest that was a natural concomitant, or so it is sometimes believed, of their radical reform attitude. On this point, too, Aelred was one of the best representatives of the monastic discipline that had attracted and formed him. A convinced Cistercian, he had a constant concern, manifested in a very human and understanding way, for the Order's observances and discipline.[138] He well knew that this discipline was austere, at times burdensome, and for the lukewarm and lax it was unbearable. He was even persuaded to take up the defense of the asceticism practiced at Cîteaux and he succeeded in integrating it with his teaching on charity.

135. *Ibid.*, 246c.
136. St Bernard, P.L. 183, 380b; Odo of Morimond, P.L. 188, 1656a; Geoffrey of Vendôme, P.L. 157, 280c.
137. *S. Temp.* VI, 247b.
138. *S. Oner.* XXIV, 463d. *Inst.* I, p. 177. *Vita*, p. 40. *Spec.* II, 17, 562a; III, 698d. See C. Dumont, *loc. cit.*, p. 177 and n. 1.

Aelred spoke from experience. Like his friend Waldef,[139] who was not robust, he must have had his periods of depression when the monastic life appeared in all its monotony, its ceaseless and dull drudgery. Even allowing for the literary genre, we gather from his description of it that the Cistercian life was considered austere even in that age which we today would regard as stern. There is nothing idyllic about these words which he puts in the mouth of one of his favorite novices: "The food is rather scanty, the clothes are quite rough; spring-water is the beverage; a book often cradles a sleepy head. Weary limbs don't make the couch any softer; the bell for rising is sure to ruin the beginnings of a good sleep. . . . We are no better than beasts of burden."[140] Walter Daniel has given us a vivid picture of a certain monk of Rievaulx who found the austerity an unbearable burden; troubled and depressed, emaciated and disgusted he let his imagination indulge in the pleasures of the world and longed to enjoy them.[141]

In a discussion with a canon regular of St Augustine[142] on the aim and scope of monastic profession, Aelred laid stress on the undeniable and intentional austerity of the Rule of St Benedict. The Benedictine observances involve "for beginners no small difficulty in such things as scant and poor food, coarse clothing, wearying vigil and fast. . . ."[143] The purifying prescriptions of our Moses are intended for our spiritual well-being: "His teaching and example are the two hands that bring us the Lord's saving help, but keeping these hands lifted up," adds Aelred, "is a weary business."[144]

The Augustinian retorted with the primacy of charity, to which Aelred replied, in no uncertain terms, that charity is precisely the

---

139. See *supra,* p. xxvii; and F. M. Powicke, Introduction to the *Vita,* p. lxxiv.

140. *Spec.* II, 17, 562d.   141. *Vita,* p. 30.

142. Published by A.Wilmart, "Un court traité d'Aelred sur l'étendue et le but de la profession monastique" in *Rev. Asc. Myst.* 23 (1947) 259–73. Dom Wilmart considers this short treatise to be prior to the *Speculum Caritatis* which contains this *Disputatio* in a more extended form (*Spec.* III, 35, 608–13).

143. *Spec.* III, 35, 612b.   144. *S. Ined.,* p. 62. Cf. Ex 17:12.

aim and ideal of the monastic life, since it is the very essence of the Christian life: "Could Benedict make one kind of charity the purpose of his Rule and Augustine teach that his Rule led to a completely different kind? Is it not rather the case that both teach the charity Christ taught by the Law and Gospel?"[145] God forbid that austerities should militate against charity. According to Aelred, some people seemed to consider them incompatible with love: "Wearing down the body with constant vigil, afflicting the flesh with daily toil, damping one's energy through using coarse food, . . . all that is so contrary to charity . . . that it not only destroys peace of mind, it makes it impossible."[146] Aelred's forceful answer to that is "Nonsense! . . . I hold the very opposite and make bold to declare that bodily mortification, for the proper reason and discreetly done, so far from hindering God-sent consolation, rather demands it."[147]

As an apologist of the Rule, the Abbot of Rievaulx re-echoes the aims of the first Cistercians: the observances are worthy of high esteem because they are devised to purify the soul and make charity grow. It could even be said that it is by holding to the letter of the Rule of St Benedict that they claim to attain its spirit. The objection is made by Dom Wilmart against Aelred's argument, which he calls a "hard Cistercian saying," that it tends, whether we like it or not, to make the means predominate in some way, in practice at least, over the end.[148] The learned Benedictine attempts to explain the hardness of Aelred's arguments by pointing to "the deliberate and disastrous severity of the Cistercian Order" and Aelred's "own character, which we think is scrupulous."[149] Aelred's practical humanism and his balanced personality—both incompatible with the narrowness of scrupulosity—would appear to dispute the truth of the assertion that he was scrupulous. And as for

---

145. *Spec.* III, 35, 610–611a.
147. *Ibid.*, 550b.
149. *Ibid.*

146. *Spec.* II, 5, 549c.
148. A. Wilmart, *art. cit.*, p. 264.

the Cistercian tendency towards a certain severity in monastic discipline, Dom Salmon suggests that if we consider it in its true historical context, we shall see it as a reaction against the contemporary monastic observance, and shall grasp the spiritual force of attachment to the observances of the Order.[150]

St Benedict handed on to his monks not simply a collection of disciplinary laws made for the smooth running of the perfect cenobitic life, but a true rule of the spiritual life, which he himself considered elementary, but which leads to sanctity when intelligently practiced. Now as a result of historical circumstances, we no longer realize the spiritual value of observances and have come to regard them as a mere system of external practices and customs, pious no doubt, but without any immediate connection with the spiritual life. Such an idea is absolutely contrary to the spirit of the Rule and the mind of St Benedict, and it is precisely the tendency against which Cîteaux and St Bernard reacted.[151] The observances have a sanctifying power since they are directed towards charity. In the school of the Lord's service set up by St Benedict, monks practice and develop charity by the means this new Moses pointed out to them. Of this Aelred is convinced. No doubt "holy canons, priests, bishops and married folk have abundant charity and for all that make no attempt to observe the Rule for monks;"[152] but for monks St Benedict is the instrument of God in the work of their sanctification. A monk who follows him with faith and is true to his prescriptions will receive from the Lord, through his fatherly mediation, all the light and strength he needs in order that charity may triumph in him.[153]

Aelred points out to the Christian, whose essential vocation is to return to God, a direct and sure way, the shortest way, appointed by St Benedict for those whom God has made his spiritual sons.

150. P. Salmon, "L'ascèse monastique et les origines de Cîteaux" in *Mélanges Saint Bernard*, Dijon, 1954, pp. 268–83, especially pp. 282–83.
151. *Ibid.*, p. 182.   152. *Spec.* III, 35, 612d.
153. *Spec.* III, 36, 613b–c.

Eruditio has only one end: the building up of souls in charity. The monastic observances in this school of Christ are not meant to hinder or cramp the soul; St Benedict saw them as the *dura et aspera*, the hardships and trials, without which the desert would be no true approach to God.

PART THREE

FEATURES OF
MONASTIC FORMATION

CHAPTER FIVE

KNOWLEDGE AND EXPERIENCE

ELRED is the master and guide of his monks, whom he teaches about God and forms in the divine way of living. We may pause here to examine the characteristic features of this monastic education of souls. What knowledge of God does a monk desire? How does he advance in the search for truth?

School of Christ and Religious Knowledge

Aelred regards the monastery as a school under the direction of Christ, in which purely intellectual knowledge is not sufficient. This school of Christ involves something more than mental speculation, valuable as this is; it calls for a disposition of soul, a love of, and desire for, the reality apprehended so as to grasp it and integrate it into one's life. In modern terminology, knowledge, if it is to be real knowledge, must lead on to personal commitment. This tendency finds constant expression in the work of the monastic theologian we are considering. We have only to listen to him speaking to his monks to be assured of it. His teaching, which was the fruit of experience, was an exhortation to gain the same experience for themselves. And the reason? There are some truths which only experience can teach.[1]

A fact or truth can be known in various ways. The mind may

---

1. S. Ined., p. 106.

adhere to a truth because of the testimony of trustworthy witnesses, and this is faith; or because it understands the reason for it, and this is science; or, finally, because of direct experience—"let thy experience teach thee."[2] These three ways lead us to give an assent of the mind which will vary according to the motive that produced it: "Belief is one thing, knowledge another, experience a third."[3]

But what kind of experience does he mean here? An experience can be had in two ways, Aelred continues: first by means of the bodily senses, and secondly by a spiritual *affectus*.[4] Between these two experiences there is a vast difference, which Aelred clearly indicates at the beginning of this same sermon when he attributes specifically different operations to the senses and the intellect, the former dealing with the *corporalia* or material things and the latter the *spiritualia* or spiritual realities.[5] Beyond doubt Aelred is speaking of a spiritual experience, a divine gift in the apex of the soul:[6] God opens his hand and fills the soul with blessing.[7] It is a spiritual perception that cannot be expressed: "spiritual experiences of which one can be aware, certainly; but explain, never."[8]

The intellect is united with an *affectus* in this kind of knowledge, which it is preferable to call "experiential" rather than "experimental," because this latter term suggests something technical. What is this element that belongs to the affective order, increases the plenitude of the intellectual act and gives it a special character? Instead of defining it at once—which might appear to be easy since Aelred gives us a definition,[9] but which would in fact be misleading, for this concept can be applied to a variety of manifestations of the affective nature—it is better to build up a description of it by showing the part it plays in spiritual knowledge and experience.

---

2. *S. Ined.*, p. 142.   3. *Ibid.*   4. *Ibid.*

5. *S. Ined.*, p. 137: *Pars inferior sensus, pars superior intellectus. . . .Sicut igitur a parte inferiori, id est, sensu judicamus inter corporalia, ita de spiritualibus intellectu discernimus.* Some lines further on, Aelred identifies *mens* and *intellectus: in mente vel intellectu imago Dei similitudoque relucet.*

6. *S. Ined.*, p. 137.   7. *S. Ined.*, p. 142.   8. *Ibid.*

9. *Spec.* III, 11, 587d; *S. Ined.*, p. 48.

Aelred was particularly interested in the study of the various human *affectus* and their psychological character. While this interest indicated a special gift of observation and introspection which the Abbot of Rievaulx possessed, it was also a current trend of his time, one of the manifestations of the new sense-awareness. "From many points of view, the twelfth century is the century of the *affectus*. . . ." The word then took on "quite a new importance and position."[10] What was Aelred's concept of *affectus?* Basically he considered it as an inclination, "a sudden, unpremeditated liking for someone."[11] The word *spontanea*, which in other contexts was used by these medieval authors to mean *voluntary*, here indicates an innate manifestation which can arise in us against our will and to the utter repugnance of our mind,[12] and which, with all its dynamic force, leads the soul to consent.[13] The *affectus* attains its human perfection when it is united with the mind and the will. Spiritual love is the highest of these *affectus* and the most perfect.[14]

The *affectus* is accompanied by pleasure, a delight that attracts or entices the soul, opens it by making it more attentive, more understanding by way of fellow-feeling. To understand something we must have a taste for it.[15] However, not every form of emotion is an advance in spiritual knowledge—far from it. We are not dealing in this context with feeling in a carnal or even sensory way, but with being "affected at the very center of one's mind."[16] Thus one acquires *sapientia*, the fruit of religious experience, such as St Bernard speaks of it in a letter to Aelred: among the trees is to be found a delightful knowledge of God that would be sought for in vain in the schools.[17] He is not talking about learning here, says Etienne Gilson,[18] or if he is, then it is a very special kind of learning.

---

10. J. Chatillon, "Cordis affectus" in *Dict. Spir.* II, col. 2291.
11. *S. Ined.,* p. 48.   12. *Ibid.* See also *Spec.* III, 19, 594c.
13. *S. Ined.,* p. 48   14. *Spec.* III, 20, 594d.
15. *S. Ined.,* p. 47.   16. *Ibid.*
17. *Epistola Bernardi ad Aelredum,* P.L. 195, 501–502.
18. E. Gilson, "Sub umbris arborum" in *Mediaeval Studies* 14 (1952) 149–51.

The very contrast between the words he uses is significant: *sub umbris arborum* senseris *quale numquam* didicisses *in scholis*. "Experience" on the one hand, and "learn" on the other. If we recall St Bernard's customary use of this word *experience*, there can be no doubt that he is thinking of a religious experience. At the same time it is suggested that the acquiring of such learning ordinarily goes hand in hand with purification of soul; illumination implies re-formation. The monk, then, is to begin his education by renouncing his own will and by the practice of an asceticism that will purify his soul: "Just as his training has brought him to right living, so his learning should lead him to wisdom."[19]

Knowledge supposes likeness; to know is to be, is to become the thing known while still remaining oneself. The union of the *affectus* and the intellect, referred to above, finds its explanation only in the doctrine of the image: the act of the intellect is accompanied by a movement of the soul that tends towards an ever truer resemblance to God and spiritual things, an inclination to possess them. This is a favorite theme of the great monastic writers of the twelfth century. St Bernard,[20] William of Saint-Thierry,[21] the Victorines[22] have repeated, in a variety of ways, that the knowledge which is wedded to love has deeper insight. It is almost connatural for a spirit of fellow-feeling to lead to understanding: "Fear has a language of its own, understood only by one who is afraid; grief

19. *S. Oner.*, 484d. These two terms *informatio* and *illuminatio* are clearly of Augustinian origin. Aelred's use of them in this context seems to suggest that *informatio* belongs to the order of being (*esse, natura*), while *illuminatio* belongs to the order of knowing. They bestow upon the soul a greater similarity to God.

20. St Bernard, *In Cantica*, serm. 67, P.L. 183, 1106c: *Res est in affectibus, nec ratione ad eam pertingitur sed conformitate.*

21. See J. M. Déchanet, *Méditations le prières de Guillaume de Saint-Thierry*, pp. 47–70.

22. Hugh of Saint-Victor, *Expositio in hierarch. coelest. S. Dionysii*, P.L. 175, 1038d. See G. Dumeige, *Richard de Saint-Victor et l'idée chrétienne de l'amour*, p. 125: "In Richard's works, knowledge is not mentioned without an immediate reference to love."

speaks a language unknown to one who does not grieve. It follows that the language of love makes sense only to one in love."[23] This knowledge, in which the *affectus* plays a part, is due to a similarity of interior state, an assimilation in the etymological sense of the word: "To understand, you must condole . . . share the joy . . . if you would perceive."[24]

When Aelred describes the experiences of the soul, he is nearly always thinking of the realm of faith. The psychological descriptions he usually gives serve chiefly as analogies. The favorite object of his study is the mysteries of faith which faith alone can disclose to us, since it alone presents them to our mind: "Faith must lead the way, open the door to understanding."[25] The task of the teacher of souls is to bring them to an even deeper understanding of the Word of God. He can then be called a "guide to the word" since by his influence the light of doctrine penetrates to the inmost recesses of the disciple's mind.[26]

The quest for knowledge, understood in this sense, is one of the elements of the return to God, the end of man. Each faculty of the soul must needs be restored. It is faith that helps the intellect to be re-orientated towards God; "the grace of faith restores the intellect."[27] Because of wisdom, the virtue that comes from on high,[28] the soul gradually recovers its beauty,[29] that is, it tends towards wisdom; "wisdom is that beauty."[30] St Bernard has a sentence that brings out perfectly the significance of all this striving for the truth that enlightens and shapes: "Teaching makes learned, love makes wise."[31] Hence Aelred's insistence is understandable. He wants his monks to desire this delightful knowledge, this spiritual learning that no human speculation can bestow, since it is a gift of God. Divine light alone can bring us understanding of divine

---

23. *S. Ined.*, p. 47.   24. *Ibid.*   25. *S. Oner.* IV, 380c.
26. *S. Oner.* IV, 380b.   27. *Spec.* I, 5, 509b.   28. *S. Oner.* VIII, 391c.
29. *S. Ined.*, p. 34; *Forma autem ipsa Dei est similitudo.*
30. *S. Oner.* I, 363c.
31. S. Bernard, *In Cant.* XXIII, 14, P.L. 183, 891d.

things: "Experience alone communicates his loving kindness; searching eye, groping hand, listening ear have no place in a sensing so spiritual as this."[32]

Aelred and the monastic writers of the twelfth century were not introducing something new, apart from a more psychological approach to the subject. They were carrying on a tradition, to some extent Platonic in character, but, as handed on by the Fathers, authentically religious. Knowledge calls for an inner disposition vis-à-vis the truth which, in the last analysis, is God. Intellectual activity for them, writes Fr I. Hausherr, did not primarily mean a world of abstractions, which any rational animal can grasp in proportion to his intelligence, and not in proportion to his moral perfection. To their way of thinking, intellectual is equivalent to spiritual and intellectual research to spiritual pursuit. To see clearly, the intellect has to be purified; then only will it grasp reality; until then, it will stop short at words and abstract concepts.[33]

Spiritual Experience

Aelred's doctrine has a very markedly concrete character, in the sense that it deals less with objective and impersonal speculation than with bearing witness to, or expressing, an experience. In it the things of the spirit are described as they have been lived by one who has encountered them, perceived them, tasted them, not indeed in a sensible way, but spiritually, by having been "affected" by them. We feel that his is a living teaching because it has been lived by him, that it takes its inspiration from life and is directed to life. It is expressed not merely in the form of definitions of essence and essential properties, but in descriptions of real life with all its incidental peculiarities. Such a doctrine holds out an invitation to

32. *S. Ined.*, p. 106.
33. I. Hausherr, "Contemplation et Sainteté" in *Rev. Asc. Myst.* 14 (1933), 184.

share that experience, a call to personal commitment, because, while it is the lawful concern of speculative research to discover what is objective, experience cannot but be personal; it brings a man, in the very depths of his soul, face to face with realities that intimately concern him.

To deny this experiential aspect of Aelred's teaching or to pass over it in silence would be to falsify it. The work of this twelfth-century monk, whose spirituality was completely influenced by *affectus*, is in no way comparable, even in its most scholarly parts, with the orderly precision and deliberately abstract language of a scholastic treatise. His daily contact with the Scriptures which brought him so much delight, the markedly affective nature of his character, the fatherly tone of his encouragement to his monks to seek God, the familiarity he had acquired with the works of St Augustine, all these united to make his work, taken as a whole, more like a personal testimony than a dogmatic or moral exposition.[34] We shall perhaps see in this living approach the essential characteristic of the theology we call monastic.[35] As a prerequisite for understanding any doctrine, a man must conform his life to it, put himself in accord with the spiritual reality he is considering: "Only a lover understands."[36] Such a disposition of soul seems to be demanded if the mind's application is to be regarded as sincere: "These things are the subject of the sermons you listen to, of the readings you do, your imaginations and minds are full of them—do not tell me that all spiritual enjoyment has passed you by."[37]

---

34. A. Le Bail, "La spiritualité cistercienne" in *Cahiers du cercle thomiste feminin* 7 (1927), says of Aelred: "The greater part of his writings forms the diary of a spiritual director." Cf. Dom Odo Brooke, "Monastic Theology and St Aelred" in *Pax* 291 (1959) 87–93.

35. J. Leclercq, "Saint Bernard et la théologie monastique de XIIᵉ siècle" in *Saint Bernard Théologien*, p. 15: "Monastic theology is thus essentially bound up with the exercise of prayer, with the practice of the contemplative life. It is founded on the 'Christian experience' described and defined by M. Mouroux . . ."

36. S. *Ined.*, p. 51.   37. S. *Ined.*, p. 49.

It is, then, a fact that Aelred often speaks of spiritual experience, but can we be more precise in stating what he means by it? It is a delicate task to determine—with all the necessary theological distinctions—the traits of a genuine Christian experience. Before we examine Aelred's definition of a spiritual experience, it is interesting and worthwhile to consider the various descriptions he gives of this "experienced" knowledge of the truths of the faith. Obviously we are venturing into a realm that remains a mystery, and the terminology of our modern psychology can be applied to it only analogically.

The experience Aelred describes is firstly a *sensus*, which in the twelfth century had a wide range of meaning; apart from sense knowledge it could also be used to express the highest spiritual activities and their principles.[38] In our present context, the *sensus* is, in fact, spiritual,[39] since it is the result of an *affectus mentis*,[40] and enriches the soul with a knowledge that is so excellent as to be preferable, in the eyes of a spiritual man, to the knowledge acquired in the schools.[41] Only one who has experienced spiritual reality can speak of it in the way experience teaches him.[42] There is, however, no adequate expression for this *sensus* which at times touches the highest part of the soul—the mind; by reason of its very intimate and spiritual character, it is simply untranslatable.[43]

At these moments a man tastes God and experiences the unique delight of heavenly things. What is this tasting of God, spoken of so frequently by monastic writers? "No one can put it into words, no, not even he to whom the experience has been granted."[44] It is perceived, it is known by the soul but it cannot be explained to

---

38. K. Rahner, "La doctrine des sens spirituels au Moyen Age" in *Rev. Asc. Myst.* 14 (1933) 265.

39. See *supra*, p. 116.   40. *S. Ined.*, p. 142.

41. *Epist. S. Bernardi*, P.L. 195, 501–502.   42. *S. Ined.*, p. 108.

43. *S. Ined.*, p. 142.

44. William of Saint-Thierry. Cf. *Oeuvres choisies de Guillaume de Saint-Thierry* . . . edited by J. M. Déchanet, p. 199.

others: "Neither mind nor tongue can convey its utter delight."[45]
However, the conviction that comes from the heart and touches the
heart can well up only from this delight experienced within us:
"Only he can tell with unction the joys of this stage who is able to
bring his terms into line with his spiritual experience."[46] To be aware
of God in such a way is the privilege of the image that has been
restored to likeness by love: "Love is the heart's palate you grant
to taste the great delight you are, loving-kind Lord. . . . To love
you is to hold you—closely in proportion to the love; you are
love . . . you the teeming plenty of which your friends drink deep . . .
by loving you, yes, unreservedly."[47] "Unreservedly"—this seems to
be an echo of St Bernard who considered the attraction this divine
delight exercises on the soul, and its purifying power, as its
characteristic mark: "the criterion of pure love is the experience of
the hidden delight of God" and "it is the tasting of the hidden
goodness of God that makes love pure."[48]

When Aelred wants to describe the encounter of a soul with God,
the visit of the Lord, he uses the language of friendship, so dear to
him. By *affectus* a man seeks God and in *affectus* he finds him:
"Jesus is touched through love."[49] William of Saint-Thierry put it
in an original way when he said that this contact that brings understanding of the Scriptures is like touching them "with the hand of
experience."[50] The more a man, under divine influence, becomes
again like to God, the more he tends with all his powers to the
divine embrace that formed man's happiness in the state of original
justice; "Memory then was a sort of embrace by which the soul
continually clung to God."[51] This loving embrace, allied to the

---

45. *S. Ined.*, p. 140.   46. *Ibid.*   47. *Spec.* I, 1, 505b-c.
48. P. Delfgaauw, "La nature et les degrés de l'amour selon saint Bernard"
in *Saint Bernard Théologien*, pp. 244-45.
49. *S. Ined.*, p. 124.
50. *Oeuvres choisies de Guillaume de Saint-Thierry*, edited by J. M. Déchanet,
p. 202. *De natura amoris* X, 31, P.L. 184, 399a.
51. *S. Ined.*, p. 38.

notion of the kiss, *osculum*, does not mean ecstasy only;[52] it is only one of the terms for a spiritual experience which is not always mystical, in the modern sense of the word. Aelred is trying to express by these words the sense of a real presence produced in the soul by the love of God: "should you sense him, your beloved, present and, so to speak, embrace him."[53]

Spiritual experience offers a twofold aspect which we may call the static and the dynamic. On the one hand, it is calm and restful, it satisfies a longing; on the other hand, it puts a keener edge on one's desire and gives a new impulse to the interior life that progresses from one experience to another. God at once fills and empties: he is love and he makes all love's demands. Love is that "tendency of the rational soul whereby it gladly seeks to enjoy something, is delighted when it obtains it and cherishes its possession."[54] The soul that has tasted God can never forget his sweetness and yearns for it: "My soul so dry, so parched, so lifeless, how it thirsts for the welcome moistening of such dew. . . . My prayer, Lord, is that some tiny share of your so great kindness come down upon my soul. . . . May it be granted some glimpse and foretaste of the true objective of its desiring, coveting, longing during its present exile."[55] Because the soul is made in God's image, the desire for him besets it; this desire was created in it by him who wishes to be sought by it: "While this present life lasts, Lord, I will keep on seeking you by loving you; who progresses in your love, he it is that seeks you."[56] God has bestowed on his image a winged love that bears it heavenward: ceaselessly, as by an impulse, this love raises us aloft towards God, "that by love and desire, with all our heart and mind we may already have our life in heaven."[57] In approaching God like this, the soul becomes more and more itself, that is, the image of God. This desire will continue to exist in

---

52. As E. Gilson seems to suggest in speaking of St Bernard; cf. *The Mystical Theology of St Bernard*, p. 104, n. 148.

53. *S. Oner.* XIII, 418c.   54. *Am.*, I, 1, ed. Dubois, pp. 14–15.

55. *Spec.* I, 1, 505c.   56. *Ibid.*, 506a.   57. *S. Ined.*, p. 35.

heaven, in the sense that there, without weariness or monotony, the soul enjoying God will never cease to be attracted by him who is everlastingly fathomless: "Ever the sight of him, never enough of it; that vision will satisfy love but it will leave longing unwearied still."[58]

One of the most desirable stages of the interior life is the Sabbath. This expression, frequently to be met with in Aelred's teaching, conjures up the thought of a sacrosanct spiritual state which the soul should make it its chief task to acquire and maintain;[59] "rest of soul, peace of heart, tranquillity of mind,"[60] such a state is a participation in the Sabbath of God who is love. Blessed the man who has attained the experience of this seventh day: "All is cheerful harmony, peace and quiet . . . ; from this springs astonishing assurance and wondering gladness and a joy that is all thanksgiving and devotion to God, so clearly does the soul perceive all its virtue to be God's free gift."[61]

Contemplation procures for a soul that leisure, *vacatio*, wherein it tastes God and which is so much desired by one who has once experienced its blessings: "If only a breathing-space were granted me . . . that for but half an hour my soul might enjoy the silence of this Sabbath."[62] When the *affectus* is thus saturated with divine delight and filled with deep peace, the soul is aware that God is restoring it to his image in a union so intimate that God who deifies and the soul who is being deified seem to become one.[63]

But better than the study of his terminology, an examination of the various spiritual experiences described by Aelred will help us to grasp his idea of them and the importance he attached to them in spiritual education. With care, psychological insight and wisdom, he observed the interior phases that characterize and mark the life

---

58. *S. Ined.*, p. 36. Here we have a favorite theme of St Gregory of Nyssa. See R. Leys, *L'image de Dieu chez saint Grégoire de Nysse*, p. 108. Similar texts are to be found in St Augustine and St Gregory the Great.

59. *Inst.* 7, p. 183.   60. *Spec.* III, 2, 577c.   61. *Spec.* III, 3, 578d.
62. *Spec.* I, 18, 521a.   63. *S. Ined.*, p. 51.

of a soul and are so many visitations of the Lord: "Would you obtain an accurate idea of the whither and wherefore of the divine visitations made to you, take, first of all, careful stock of the stage you have reached and of your life and behavior; using, not some chance reckoning of your own, but the standards laid down by the Scriptures and the conditions established by the heavenly precepts, and the obligations of your state of life; make a conscientious and close examination."[64]

In some of his descriptions where he speaks with deep conviction, it is hard to avoid the impression that Aelred is describing his own experiences.[65] In other passages he explicitly uses the first person singular. He thus describes his experience of wretchedness in his youth, when he was seeking happiness where it was not to be found: "With such things did I seek rest . . . but all was labor lost and lamentation, grief and pain. . . . There I lay, filthy and bewildered, a prisoner in chains, stuck fast in the clinging mire of sin, in thrall to the burden of long habit. So when I came to myself ... I was horrified at my condition. I was disgusted with myself, for you were beginning to delight me."[66] When writing to his sister, Aelred, perhaps by way of contrast with the purity which this virgin symbolized for him, depicts certain incidents of his youth in the style, and at times even in the very words, of St Augustine: "What wretchedness was mine once I lost my innocence . . . You have but to recall your grief over my aberrations. . . . What time lust like a thick cloud rose from that marsh of carnality . . . and my excesses brooked no restraint."[67]

A digression introduced into the *Mirror of Charity* is worth studying, for it is an analysis of a spiritual experience taken from life, in this instance the life of a novice.[68] The passage is instructive because of the psychological problem treated in it and also because it reveals Aelred's method of guiding souls. This young novice

---

64. *Spec.* II, 14, 558b-c.
65. See G. Coulton, *Five Centuries of Religion,* I, p. 356.
66. *Spec.* I, 28, 531c.   67. *Inst.* 32, p. 210.   68. *Spec.* II, 17-20, 562-569.

came and confided to him his pained surprise: when he was in the world, he often felt full of compunction, as if his soul were "quite dissolved in love of God"; his spiritual life was one of almost continual sweetness.[69] But now, in the cloister, he suffers from dryness, no longer tasting the delight of heavenly consolations. He recalls his religious experiences in the world when he "loved" God so fervently, and cannot understand why he has not similar "devotion" in the monastery. We are then allowed to listen to a dialogue between the experienced monk and the worried novice. Aelred gradually leads him to an understanding of God's ways and teaches him how to discern the stages of the spiritual life. It is a maieutic investigation, after the fashion of Socrates, that leaves the pupil the joy of discovering the truth for himself and has the advantage of training his judgment.

"Do you consider your former life more holy and pleasing to God than this?" The novice readily acknowledges the austerity of his present life and paints an enthusiastic and idyllic picture of life at Rievaulx. He cannot but conclude that such a way of life is perfect: "Our way of life and its obligations seem to me to lack absolutely nothing of the perfection taught by the evangelists and apostles, by the holy Fathers or the first monks."[70] And yet he recalls anew his former consolations; then, he muses, "ever so often was it granted me to feel the strength and kindness of Christ's love for me";[71] "my love for God was greater then."[72] Aelred uses great tact in helping him to see his state of soul clearly and to gauge the value of his spiritual experiences: "Tell me, in all honesty and according to your conscience, where your preference lies: is it with your former state or with this?"[73]

The novice declares his preference for his present state, adding that it is only the love of Christ that keeps him in his austere vocation. However, he still makes much of, and is impressed by,

---

69. *Spec.* II, 17, 562b. 70. *Ibid.,* 563b. 71. *Ibid.,* 562b.
72. *Ibid.,* 563d. 73. *Ibid.,* 564a.

the fact that in the world he felt God's love more keenly; this is a fact of experience which cannot be denied. "I cannot have the slightest doubt that then my love for God was greater, if experience proves anything and the fact that the mere thought of his love had me so often in tears."[74] Aelred's advice to him is to beware of his feelings: to be aware of one's feelings is one thing, to estimate their worth quite another; experience can be deceptive.[75] It is not enough simply to feel some experience, we must be able to judge its meaning and importance. Now feelings are not the norm for judging the genuineness of a Christian experience: "The first thing you must learn is that such transitory and, if I may say so, such momentary love, is no measure of one's love for God."[76]

These emotions are not under the control of our will.[77] Sometimes they are "given, so to say, arbitrarily to such as do not look for them, while those who make every effort to obtain them are left without them."[78] The true criterion of our love for God is the submission of our will to his, especially in the painful circumstances of life or in the practices of an austere way of living: "To so join one's will to God's will that one's will seconds every lead of God's will, that it chooses only what it knows for God's will: here indeed is loving God."[79]

The novice learned the lesson. The youth, who formerly tasted so much consolation in loving God, was even more emotionally affected and moved to tears when he read the tales of King Arthur. He realized now that feelings are no true sign of loving God: "One man really loves, yet does not feel he does; another feels he does, while really he does not."[80] "Were such feelings the measure of our love . . . we must say that our love is spasmodic, a case of 'now and then'."[81]

Aelred, however, would not have the novice condemn or minimize the spiritual experiences he had in the world. They formed

---

74. *Ibid.*, 564c.   75. *Ibid.*, 564d.   76. *Ibid.*, 565b.
77. *Spec* II, 18, 566b.   78. *Ibid.*, 566d.   79. *Ibid.*, 566b.
80. *Ibid.*, 567b.   81. *Spec.* II, 18, 567a.

part of God's plan for him, God's way of teaching him. Monastic conversion is "in its way, the consequence of those tears. . . . God was using them. Nothing strange if they have ceased with their function."[82] Henceforth in a more perfect state of life God expects proof of a more perfect love, such as "to suffer for Christ, to exercise patience . . . to be put to the test repeatedly . . . to deny your own liking."[83]

We have to admire the skill with which Aelred handled and solved this spiritual problem which perplexes many people, who, on coming out of Egypt, are discouraged by their first experience of the desert.[84] He showed talent as a teacher in the way he led his novice to a knowledge of himself and God's way of dealing with him. The latter is now delighted with the light that has been shed on his life and his inner experiences: "Your words are welcome to me, very welcome . . . their truth is clearer than light to me. My experience of the first kind of grace you have mentioned has been exactly as you say; only lately have I become aware of the second kind, which your account helps me to recognize; as for that lofty, indescribable third kind, I have strong hope of attaining it some day."[85]

All through his religious life a monk will have to maintain and foster the desire for true spiritual experience. Responsive to God's influence, he will go to meet him, will move from one experience to another. Sometimes these experiences will be full of unction, at other times dry. The most favorable times for these visitations from heaven are ordinarily the times of the spiritual exercises of the monastic life: *lectio divina*, the celebration of the liturgy and private prayer. Aelred is insistent in urging his monks to the *vacatio* of the soul, the peace and joy that only God can give.[86]

---

82. *Spec.* II, 19, 568b.   83. *Ibid.*, 568c.
84. L. Bouyer, *The Cistercian Heritage*, p. 139: "This problem, which Aelred analyzed and resolved with his usual psychological acumen, was a new one."
85. *Spec.* II, 19, 568d–569a.   86. *S. Ined.*, p. 117.

L

As we have already said,[87] the spiritual understanding of the Scriptures, that insight beyond the letter, is an experience. The monastic writers are seeking Someone present in their *lectio divina*. Their mystical approach to Scripture leads them to desire contact with the living God. His Word is a message of love for each soul, and the Spirit, who inspired it, adapts it, as he pleases, to each one's capacity.[88] This brings light to the soul and this unction makes it understand—*intus-legere*—God's graciousness more by the heart than by the reason. The monk makes his way, by constant meditation, through the field of Scripture, and, like a bee that gathers honey from many flowers, he produces in his heart wonderful delight and heavenly sweetness.[89]

The experiential aspect of contact with the Bible is something that has always been known and aspired to by every spiritual man seeking God. Cassian has an excellent passage on the subject where he urges monks to re-live what they read in Scripture, to such an extent that it becomes the expression of their own experience. What the prophet of old spoke of "takes place day by day in them."[90] Aelred repeats these words of Cassian and believes that the holy Scriptures contain the secret of each one's spiritual progress: "It may be granted to me to explain the Gospel text and your progress all in one; that so you may read in these pages the story of your own experience."[91]

Fully convinced of this truth, a monk concentrates his attention

87. See *supra,* p. 92.
88. *S. Oner.* XIX, 438d. Cf. *S. Oner.* I, 363d.
89. *S. Temp.* XIX, 320c-d.
90. J. Cassian, *Collat.* 10, c. 11: "Never ceasing to partake of this life-giving food (of Scripture) he so enters into the sentiments expressed in the psalms that he recites them no longer as if they were composed by the Prophet but as if he himself were the author.... At any rate, he feels they were made for him; and he realizes that what they speak of, has not been experienced solely in the person of the Prophet but is fulfilled every day in himself." (See E. Pichery, Introduction to Cassian's *Conférences* in *Sources chrétiennes,* no. 42, p. 50.)
91. *Jesu,* 19, P.L. 184, 861a-b.

on the mystery or sacrament of the biblical narrative. The spiritual path he must tread is there, indicated in an obscure way. The life of Christ reveals it to us, his mysteries are renewed in us: "His bodily growth is the exemplar of our spiritual progress to such an extent that what we read of his development is experienced step by step, spiritually, by those who go steadily forward."[92]

Very often it is while celebrating the liturgy that the grace of spiritual insight into the Scriptures comes to the monk: in the rhythm of the psalmody, a light breaks in on him that penetrates the deep-reaching meaning of the Word of God.[93] The liturgical mysteries are themselves the object of interior experience. When the divine unction, hidden in the symbolic actions, is revealed to us and touches the "heart's discernment," then the soul has a closer participation in the economy of salvation proclaimed by, and accomplished through, the liturgy.[94]

At time of prayer, when the soul communes alone with God, it experiences a variety of *affectus* under the influence of the Holy Spirit: "Who can tell the manifold affections of a soul in prayer?"[95] At times the soul groans beneath the burden of its sins, at other times it recalls God's immense graces and so its mood changes from fear to hope, from compunction to desire. When it is buoyed up with confidence, it is well aware that this is not produced by its own efforts, but that God infuses the Spirit of his Son into it at these moments.[96]

There are various degrees and forms of spiritual experience. A real encounter with God can be experienced without its being marked by any sign of unusual intensity. On the other hand, there are some states that human language is incapable of describing: "In this case nothing is more grateful than silence."[97] When the stains of the soul's sins have been washed away, and useless affections have been stilled within it, when it is no longer agitated by the least

92. *Jesu*, 11, P.L. 184, 856b-c.   93. *Inst.* 32, p. 212.
94. *S. Ined.*, pp. 104, 106, 112.   95. *S. Oner.* V, 383b.
96. *Ibid.*, 383b-c.   97. *S. Ined.*, p. 51.

desire for temporal things, nor tossed about on the surging stream of its thoughts, then God unites such a soul to himself. Swallowed up in the Lord as in a deep abyss, the soul feels that it becomes but one, in this spiritual kiss, with him whom it loves: "Created spirit and the Uncreated, each meets the other and they so unite that they become not merely two in one but one thing only."[98] "In this light past all description, in delight so extraordinary . . . all else is quiet; things visible, things perceptible, whatever is at the mercy of change, all such is quiet, while the hungry mind fixes its gaze on what truly is and is ever such, the Being, the Unique. In such stillness it sees that the Lord is God, as in the tenderness of his loving embrace it rests in the Great Sabbath rest."[99]

In one of his sermons[100] Aelred gives a definition of an authentic Christian experience, which it is instructive to examine. It is an *anointing* by the Holy Spirit, with all that this word suggests of God's permeating sweetness and influence in the human soul.[101] It is an *interior testimony* to the fact of our privilege as children of God, that is, a sharper awareness that we are God's image, shaped to *the* Image, the only-begotten Son of the Father. It is a *foretaste* of our future beatitude.[102] It brings light and warmth to our heart, and a knowledge that owes its clear-sightedness to the love that accompanies it, a love that sees and tastes, a heart that ponders and understands. Christian experience thus involves the whole person—intellect, will and senses.[103] Produced by God, it has its effects upon the theological virtues: it gives conviction to our faith, it strengthens our hope, it fosters charity.

---

98. S. *Ined.*, pp. 51–52.   99. *Spec.* III, 6, 583a.

100. S. *Oner.* XXI, 451c: *Est quaedam in hac vita experientia, quae fidem probat, spem corroborat, nutrit caritatem; unctio scilicet illa spiritus, quae nos docet de omnibus; quae quasdam nobis futurae beatitudinis infundit primitias, cor nostrum simul illuminans et accendens, ut videat et amet et gustet et intelligat; quando ipse spiritus testimonium reddit spiritui nostro, quoniam sumus filii Dei* (Cf. Rom ch. 8).

101. See also *Jesu,* P.L. 184, 851a.

102. Cf. *Spec.* II, 11, 556b; S. *Temp.* XIX, 320c.

103. J. Mouroux, *The Christian Experience,* translated by G. Lamb, p. 8.

Spiritual experience comes from the Spirit; it is not the result of human efforts, yet it does require on our part a preparation, a purification. If our *affectus* do not rise above the carnal, we shall not taste divine things.[104] No one enters the various temples of God without first undergoing death in some sense. It is true to say that for each experience of a higher degree there has to be a correspondingly greater purification.[105]

All Christian life involves some experience of God and there could be no faith in the living God without some *affectus* of the entire soul. The divine image in us is not a question of merely knowing, it is much more a question of loving, and so of striving for possession, for enjoyment, for union. Now it is a historical fact that monastic spirituality has always been preoccupied with the desire "to know and to grasp by experience the kingdom of God within oneself."[106] Subject, of course, to a variety of degrees and interpretations, the aim of monasticism as a whole may be said to be experiences of this kind.[107] What we have noted in Aelred's teaching is confirmed by other studies on the monastic theology of the writers of the twelfth century, a theology which "is, in a way, founded on a charter of charity; the *affectus*, the attraction a man experiences for his God is the starting-point and condition of all Christian speculation, as it is its terminus and fruit."[108]

The study of spiritual experience in Aelred brings us back, then, to the doctrine of the image, the basis of the education he gave his monks. A human soul, the image of God, is "affected" by an innate inclination towards its exemplar. Moving from one experience to another, it gradually achieves its fulfillment as a likeness of God, and the supreme experience of the beatific vision and ultimate possession of God will coincide with the soul's perfect restoration

104. *S. Ined.*, p. 128. Cf. *S. Oner.* XXVIII, 484d; *S. Oner.* XXXI, 500a.
105. *S. Ined.*, p. 128.
106. Nicephorus, quoted by I. Hausherr in *Or. Christ. Per.* 20 (1954) 25.
107. I. Hausherr, *ibid.*, p. 10.
108. J. Leclercq, in *Saint Bernard Théologien*, p. 14.

to the divine likeness: "The purpose of the efforts, of the trouble I have taken, the very heart of my intent is that the loving sight of him may transform us into the closest possible likeness to him."[109]

109. *S. Ined.*, p. 137.

CHAPTER SIX

COMMUNITY LIFE

WHILE the monastic formation aimed at by Aelred is something personal and directed to the development of the monk's personality, it is never individualistic. A monk forms part of a community that offers him help and requires him to act in a community spirit. His neighbor is always included in the perspective of his return to God: it is a return as a body, as a people. The mind and teaching of the Abbot of Rievaulx and his treatment of his monastic family are pervaded by this altruistic outlook— altruistic in the Christian sense of the word—by this awareness of the presence at our side of others united in the same spiritual purpose, by this compactness of the whole, this faith in the solidarity of all the sons of God.

After showing that the return to God takes place in a community of salvation—what might be called biblical and monastic ecclesi- ology—we shall explain how the reason for this is to be found in human nature as well as in the divine plan. The very law of human nature, which is love, has an essentially social character; there is no true love without the coordination of the love of God, love of self and love of neighbor; there can be no true beatitude in isolation from others. Man is restless while he is alone; he makes no progress when he is not in communion with others.

The Monastic Community: A Community of Salvation

The study of this community aspect must begin with Scripture.

135

We have seen[1] that, as a result of Aelred's acquaintance with the inspired books, his view of the whole enterprise of returning to God was colored by the Scriptural narrative. Monks, like the Israelites under the leadership of Moses, are en route to the promised land with St Benedict as their lawgiver and leader: "Loving-kind Lord, is not this your household, your chosen people brought by you a second time out of Egypt."[2] Using this very incident of the Exodus as the starting-point for his comments in a sermon for the feast of St Benedict, Aelred stresses the community aspect of life in a monastery. The reason he gives for this is that such is God's design.[3] In his *Pastoral Prayer* the same view of monastic life is found: "You have brought them together from all around and enable them live in community in this house."[4]

The community of salvation, God's chosen people on the march, of whom Holy Scripture speaks, is the Church, the model and setting of the monastic community. The Church, the fulfillment of the mystery of Christ, is ever envisaged in the Scriptures, hence the profound meaning of the spiritual understanding of the Bible: history has but one meaning, it has unity and continuity in the mind of God. The business of spiritual men is to discover the main features of the divine preparation, that is, the utterances of the prophets, and to show how these find their fulfillment in the Church: "God's Word commemorates the past, penetrates the present, declares the future."[5]

Interpreted allegorically, salvation history reveals the mystery of the Church, the Old Testament foretelling and prefiguring the

---

1. See *supra*, pp. 71–78.

2. *O. Past.*, 3; *Auteurs. . .* , p. 292.

3. *S. Temp.* VII, 249b: *pia dispensatione.* This important theme is developed in the course of the present chapter.

4. *O. Past.*, 3; *Auteurs . . .* , p. 292.

5. *S. Ined.*, p. 31.

Church of Christ that was manifested in the New.[6] It is enough to read the sermons *De Oneribus* to realize this. We would not grasp the meaning of this commentary and would little appreciate the thoughts it contains if we did not see it primarily as a meditation on the prophecies of Isaiah in the light of their fulfillment in the history of the Church.[7] Over and over again we find such expressions as: "This takes place daily in holy Church."[8] The Church, God's chosen people, is in fact one, and takes in the whole of biblical history; she includes within her fold all righteous men "from Abel to the holy man who latest appears in this world."[9] There is only one Bride of Christ; the story of the Bible is the account of the Son of God's countless overtures of love for this Bride of his choice, whom he had to redeem and purify: "Before the world began she was already chosen and predestined . . . he chose her and loved her . . ."[10]

From the creation of man to the end of the world, therefore, a community of salvation is on the march towards God, who is ever pursuing it with his love and accomplishing his saving plan in it. The whole story of its progress is centered in Christ and is summed

6. J. Chatillon has brought out this point well in his study of the ecclesiology of the Victorines: "Une ecclésiologie médiévale: l'idée de l'Eglise dans la théologie de l'école de Saint-Victor au XIIe siècle" in *Irenikon* 22 (1949) 115–38, 395–411. He says, for example, in a note on p. 130: "In fact the quest of the allegorical sense leads almost inevitably to Christ or the Church. . . the allegorical sense is most frequently an ecclesiological sense"; and on p. 132: "The Church's inmost nature and essence can be truly reached only by this way of symbolism so often used in the Middle Ages, and nowhere more necessary than here."

7. In *Sermon IX*, for example, col. 401b–c. Aelred finds in Isaiah, *propheta doctus in Spiritu*, the declaration of various phases of the Church's history: *primum de apostolorum praedicatione*; *postea de Ecclesiae persecutione*; *deinde de gentium conversione, et pacis tranquillitate, et sic de lapsorum poenitentia et mortis terrore*; *postremo de tempore Antichristi, et retributione justorum, et malorum condemnatione . . .*

8. See for example S. *Temp.* I, 215b, and S. *Oner.* IX, 396c.

9. S. *Temp.* X, 269d and S. *Ined.*, p. 43.

10. S. *Ined.*, p. 40.

up in his two comings. The yearning that filled the righteous men of the Old Law for Christ's bodily coming should also make us long for his glorious coming.[11] Every human being accomplishes his return to God and effects the restoration of the divine image in himself within this community. There is no individual but achieves his destiny in the Church. The monastic family, which is organized for the precise purpose of returning to God more surely,[12] is clearly in line with this ecclesiology of the Bible. The *transitus* is a community enterprise. The man who wants to achieve his salvation with greater security embarks on the strongly built and excellent ship of the monastery;[13] or again, takes refuge in the fortified city of the monastic state so as to resist successfully the attacks of the enemies of salvation.[14] The peace that prevails in this society appears to Aelred as the fulfillment of one of the messianic prophecies.[15] Integrated into this society, a monk shares in the common task of seeking God. Like the holy tent that was Yahweh's dwelling and moved about with the chosen people, the monastic family is journeying with God. God is in it, but all its members must collaborate in the journey of this tent through the desert.[16]

The community aspect of the monastic life is very strongly emphasized in the teaching of the Abbot of Rievaulx. We may wonder whether this should be ascribed to his own personality, because he had a special gift of sympathy and thoughtfulness for others, or to the grace of his abbatial state. For whatever reason it was always one of the chief points on which he laid stress. In the monastery the common life is a matter of duty and wisdom; it makes very searching demands; it is a source of concord; it achieves

11. *S. Temp.* I, 210–211.   12. See *supra*, p. 68.
13. *S. Temp.* XIX, 317b.   14. *S. Oner.* X, 405a.
15. *S. Temp.* I, 215b, 215d.
16. *S. Temp.* VII, 248a-b: *Adhuc autem tabernaculum, quia (Dominus) peregrinatur in vobis, esurit in vobis, sitit in vobis. S. Ined.,* p. 146. The theme of the Tabernacle is met with frequently in medieval exegesis. See M.-D. Chenu, "Théologie symbolique et exégèse scolastique" in *Mélanges Joseph de Ghellinck,* t. II, pp. 512–13.

the cooperation of all for the common good and offers mutual enrichment: "One is able to offer more toil, another more vigil or more fasting, more prayer or more *lectio* . . . as (in the account of Exodus) all contributed to the construction of a single tabernacle . . . so, in our case, all is to be done for the good of the community. . . . No one is to behave as though the gift he has received from God were merely for his own use. . . . No, he must regard it as belonging to all his brethren. On the other hand, he cannot envy his brother if he is convinced that he benefits through whatever gift his brother has."[17] It is not just a question of giving mutual help suggested by human prudence or by the experience of our individual weakness; rather, these services are part of God's purpose, of his plan for our salvation: "It is certainly not beyond almighty God to grant instant perfection to everyone and bestow all the virtues on each of us, but his loving arrangement for us is that we should need one another."[18]

Christian solidarity turns the social body itself into praise of God, and bears witness to the inner vital principle that constitutes its unity and equilibrium: "For in this way, humility is kept safe, charity grows, unity is made manifest."[19] There must be no room for boasting or jealousy: "Each one's gift belongs to the community and each one shares in all that the community offers. . . . So the lay-brethren are not to complain that they offer less of chant and vigils than the choir-brethren. The choir-brethren, in their turn, are not to be reproached for doing less labor than the lay-brethren. The truth of the matter is that each one contributes to the good of all and each one benefits by all the good done."[20] Such a truth can only be founded on faith, and indeed Aelred recalls St Paul's comparison of our unity in Christ, which makes us members of one another (Rom 12:5).

The Abbot of Rievaulx was obviously at pains to make this

---

17. *S. Temp.* VII, 249a.
18. *Ibid.*, 249b.
19. *Ibid.*, 249b.
20. *Ibid.*, 249b–c.

community spirit prevail in his monastery. We catch echoes of it at least in his contemporaries and those who benefited by this spirit. Walter Daniel admired the equality which appeared to be the common law for all: "Little and great, young and old, lettered and unlettered, all are subject to the same law."[21] Scarcely had a novice arrived at Rievaulx than he was immediately struck by the community atmosphere: "So great is the community and unanimity of the brethren that no one seems to have anything of his own, while each one seems to own the whole place. What strikes me most favorably is that there are no preferences; high birth does not count. The needs and infirmities of individuals are the only sources of difference and exception."[22]

In this way the monastic community becomes a family, instead of being a fortuitous gathering where each one would gradually install himself and establish for himself a niche that would afford him class distinction, occupation and honor in this small, restricted circle in which vanity would still succeed in obtaining some measure of satisfaction. Such a tendency was constantly opposed by Aelred. Where there is harmony and unity, the good of each one is no longer solely what is good for himself, but what contributes to the good of all.[23] Each one's virtue must be at the service of the whole community. Those who have received more from God must come to the aid of the others, for they have received these gifts not for themselves only, but for those who have less.[24] In the unity of the monastic community provision is made for necessary differences in order that everything may be in order and at peace in the house of God. Aelred reminds officials of their duties, points out their responsibilities and the dangers that can befall them. All are to be mindful of the common good and not of their personal interests; each one is to do his particular duty loyally so that the fortified castle may be defended against all its enemies.[25]

21. *Vita*, p. 12.   22. *Spec.* II, 17, 563a.   23. *S. Temp.* XXIII, 347c.
24. *Ibid.*, 347d–348a.   25. *S. Temp.* XV, 295b.

Some are to be specially careful of regular observance and avoid idle curiosity and laxity; others will take care of the community's duty of showing charity to the poor and to guests, and these will have to beware of avarice and miserly sadness in parting with their alms; superiors must be the guardians of justice and discipline, while fearing lest they themselves become vain or proud.[26]

This fellowship of Christians finds one of its most beautiful expressions when monks, gathered together in their church, vie with one another in fervor at the *Opus Dei*, and their praise then rises to heaven as one single flame in which all are united.[27]

The cenobitic demands of Cistercian life form part of Aelred's program of monastic education. As the company with whom we journey through the desert, as the setting of our spiritual experiences, the milieu in which our return to God takes place, as a church within the Church, the monastic community recalls to us the essentially social character of our Christian life, the basic truth that men are instruments for the sanctification of their fellows, and the unity of the children of God is realized in and through Christ.

The Community Law: Serving One Another

The community spirit demanded of a monk in all his activity is not simply a modality inherent in the cenobitic character of Cistercian life, though it is attributed to this more often than not. It has an essentially Christian signification, namely, that to be mindful of others is a sign and effect of our orientation towards God. In Aelred's teaching, there is to be found a theology of the common life, less developed no doubt than in Baldwin of Ford,[28] but which fits into the totality of his doctrine on man and God with remarkable consistency. In turning back on itself by sinning, the image

26. *Ibid.*, 295–96.
27. *S. Oner.* V, 382d.
28. Baldwin of Ford, *De vita communi*.

shut itself up from God,[29] from fellow creatures and from itself; when conversion directs the image anew to its exemplar, it finds itself again and opens itself to its neighbor and to God.[30] In the land of unlikeness, the soul was alone and selfishly thought only of itself. Returning to the family of God, it is restored to unity and becomes one heart and one soul with all God's children.[31]

The source of unity and solidarity of all creatures is creative Love who "by the unswerving and unfathomable transcendence of its presence, controls, enfolds, penetrates all things, uniting them no matter how they differ . . . giving each a share in assured peace."[32] "He, the Highest, created whatever exists, assigning each its place in the scheme of things, determining its particular duration. His plan was . . . that all creation should be at one and in peace, reflecting, though faintly, the unity of the sovereignly absolute Being. Hence nothing has been left in isolation."[33] When all things, each in its own time and place, remain in the tranquillity of order, united to one another by mutual solidarity, they find their rest and their happiness: "Out of their place they find disquiet, in it they rest."[34]

But in the case of God's favored creatures made in his image, their solidarity tends to become communion in imitation of the divine unity, and it is the Holy Spirit who achieves this most intimate spiritual union. Within the Blessed Trinity he is the bond of the Father and the Son, their Love "and the consubstantial unity of both;"[35] in the family of Christians, it is likewise he who "brings it about that there should be one heart and soul in all of you,"[36] because he is Love and infuses love into us, love that is the unifying force par excellence, for which "there is no such thing as high and low," and which can harmonize diverse elements and "bridge the greatest differences."[37]

---

29. *Spec.* I, 7, 512a.
31. *S. Temp.* XXIII, 347a-b.
33. *Am.*, I, 667a-b, ed. Dubois, p. 34.
35. *Spec.* I, 20, 523c.
37. *Epist. ad Gilbertum*, P.L. 195, 361–362.

30. *S. Ined.*, p. 57.
32. *Spec.* I, 21, 524a-b.
34. *Spec.* I, 21, 524c.
36. *S. Temp.* XXIII, 347b.

Every man of noble character loves and desires communion with
other people so that both he and they may benefit by the mutual
interchange and enrichment. In this tendency Aelred sees not merely
a natural instinct but discovers in it a gracious design of God.
God willed that, in imitation of the life of the Blessed Trinity, which is
an interchange surpassing human description, men on earth should
be in continual relationship with one another by mutual acts of
kindness, through which creatures exhibit a likeness to the divine
goodness.[38] This interchange is so advantageous that it will condition even our happiness in the next life; our end is God, but it
involves a relationship with the other elect as well. This idea seemed
to appeal to Aelred's affectionate heart: man's perfect beatitude
means communion in the happiness of others. In heaven the object
of our enjoyment will be, in a sense, twofold—God and our
neighbor, though in different ways: we shall enjoy God in and for
himself, we shall enjoy our neighbor in God, or rather, we shall
enjoy God in him.[39]

If every form of Christian life, precisely because it is life in Christ,
is social in its deep-reaching spiritual reality, the cenobitic life is so
in a very explicit manner—in the idea behind it, in its organization
and in the ideal it sets before those who embrace it, namely, that
of a body of men striving for the same goal by way of the same
means. When the monastic life is seen in this light, its community
character stands out as of primary importance. In a more pronounced way than in the ordinary Christian life, this way of life
offers monks the opportunity to meet all the demands of fraternal
charity and to fight against the faults that are a constant obstacle to
the full flowering of this virtue.

---

38. *S. Ined.*, p. 108: *Deus, itaque, licet sit sufficiens bonum sibi, abundantiam
tamen bonitatis suae extendit ad creaturam, sibi detrahens et utilitatem omnibus
conferens. Sed quia anima rationalis Deo nil conferre potuit, creati sunt ejusdem
naturae plures, ut in hac etiam parte similitudo divinae bonitatis, quae refunderet in
multos, mutuis beneficiis appareret.*

39. *Spec.* III, 9, 587a.

The rectifying of the divine image in us leads necessarily to an opening out to the other images of God. As Aelred saw it, there is a logical connection between the two. When studying his teaching on charity and friendship, we noted that the deep-reaching process of Christian maturation, spoken of by Canon J. Leclercq,[40] which transforms a man's spiritual views in the sense of unifying the two loves, begins early. Aelred has some excellent things to say about the coordination of the three loves, namely, love of self, of others and of God,[41] and there is an organic connection between the commencement, the growth and the flowering of these three.[42] These three loves, "though, obviously, different, yet so amazingly dovetail into one another that not only is each found in all of them and all in each, but where you have one there you have all, and should one fail, all fail."[43] Aelred explains this connection of the three loves as follows: "Who loves neither neighbor nor God, does not love himself. Who does not love himself, loves not his neighbor as himself. Lastly, who does not love his neighbor proves he does not love God."[44] Why? Because there is no true love of self, that is, an *ordered* love, without some initial love of God: "A man's true love for himself begins when he begins to love God."[45] Similarly it is necessary to have some seed of divine love in oneself if one is to love other men truly as one's brothers.

Love of God determines, and at the same time, perfects the other two, for it is the life and soul of them: "This love, no matter how imperfect, must precede love both of self and of neighbor; otherwise, these are lifeless and, consequently, non-existent. Yes, it does seem to me that love of God is the very soul of the other two; living itself, giving life by its presence; its absence bringing death."[46]

Aelred, the theologian of spiritual friendship, ventures the opinion that to love men thus in God is to exercise the divine attributes towards them. To experience the delight of a friend is "to delight

---

40. J. Leclercq, *La vocation religieuse*, p. 221.
41. See *supra*, pp. 50-52.   42. *Spec.* III, 2, 578b.   43. *Ibid.*, 577d.
44. *Ibid.*   45. *Ibid.*, 578a.   46. *Ibid.*

in him *in the Lord.*"[47] What is the meaning of the phrase *in the Lord*? The Lord is our wisdom, our justification, our sanctification:[48] "To delight in the Lord is to delight wisely, with restraint, justly. Wisdom gives no place to worldly nonsense; restraint keeps the flesh in subjection: justice allows no complicity or flattery."[49] The divine image appears most clearly in a monk's community activity. The ideal of this community life is the Sabbath of fraternal charity, when a soul experiences how good it is for brothers to live together: "There a man discovers that he is united by the bond of love to all his brethren . . . when he enfolds and cherishes all with such kindly affection that he makes but one heart and soul with them."[50]

But this fraternal love, which is soothing as oil, is not an ideal that is easy of attainment for men more or less in the grip of deep-rooted selfishness, cupidity. Self-will is ever impeding or destroying communion with others: "Our loving . . . banefully poisoned by selfishness, wretchedly caught in the clinging mire of pleasure, is ever drawn downwards by its own weight."[51] Aelred is forceful and emphatic in denouncing the vices that stem from selfishness—envy and suspicion—which, like noxious flies, are liable to destroy all peace within us.[52] The heart of an envious man has no rest; wrapped up in himself, he withers away in his bitterness.[53]

Charity, on the other hand, opens the eyes of the soul to the true interests of one's neighbor and stirs up in the heart the good zeal recommended by St Benedict. A friend has a sense of responsibility for his neighbor's spiritual progress, and regards fraternal correction as a duty of friendship: "In the first place, let them be concerned for one another . . . let each grieve over his friend's shortcomings as he would over his own, consider his friend's progress as his own."[54] In a monastery, all the members of the religious family must have a sense of mutual responsibility and give mutual support to one

47. According to St Paul, Philemon 20. 48. I Cor 1:30.
49. *Spec.* III, 40, 619d.   50. *Spec.* III, 4, 579b–c.   51. *Spec.* I, 8, 512c.
52. *S. Temp.* VII, 249c.   53. *S. Ined.*, p. 72. Cf. *S. Ined.*, pp. 60 and 141.
54. *Am.*, III, 695a, p. 170.

M

another. The strong are to help the weak, those who are spiritual support the "lame," as Aelred calls those discontented monks whose observance goes limping, who are "quick to grumble, wearied by everything . . . lazy at work, ever fond of trifling . . . shameless in their selfishness, bitter in their silence."[55] Fervent monks will be found always ready to help them on by advice and encouragement, by exhortation and correction, and, above all, by their prayers, until these sickly souls, cured by God, rise up out of themselves and go forward singing the praises of the Lord.[56]

When, following Aelred's directives, a perfect community spirit is achieved, it solves, in a practical way, the problem of two apparent incompatibilities in one and the same heart: namely, a love of neighbor that tends to have preferences in the form of friendships, and, at the same time, extends itself to include the entire human race. Certainly friendship with all men is not possible on earth; there are innumerable and insurmountable obstacles to it; besides, that would no longer be friendship, as we ordinarily understand it, and yet, one day, in the family life of heaven, our friendship "will be poured out on all." Why? Because then "God will be all in all" (1 Cor 15:28).[57] Indeed the more a soul becomes like to God, the more spiritual and universal becomes its love. To the monk in his cloister Aelred confides the care of all men: "Take the whole world to your loving heart. Think of honest folk and rejoice; of the wicked and grieve. Pity those in any way afflicted and depressed: the wretched poor, the lonely orphan, the helpless widow, the unsuccored mourner, the homeless vagrant, the discontented maiden; the peril of those at sea, the temptations of monks. . . ."[58]

The community character of monastic life is a salient feature of Aelred's doctrine on charity, the essence of his teaching. Charity tends towards union, it seeks unity. It restores this unity in each soul by directing its love towards God and by combating the disorder

55. *S. Ined.*, p. 128.   56. *Ibid.*
57. *Am.*, III, 702b, p. 201.   58. *Inst.*, 28, p. 199.

and division caused by cupidity. It re-establishes the harmony that sin destroyed, concord with God, the angels and other men. It achieves the unification of our affections and brings them to focus on God: "That divine fire, growing ever warmer, absorbs, as though they were mere sparks, those other loves and transfers the soul's entire affection to the supreme and immense Good . . . bringing all to God."[59]

Only God, in fact, can unify his creatures to such a degree by uniting them to himself. The union of the divine will and the human will is accomplished by his Holy Spirit who is substantial Love: "The Holy Spirit, God's very will and love, God himself, comes and pours himself out in our hearts, lifting their affection to such heights, so completely transforming it into something that shares his own mode and intensity that it is not a mere clinging to him, be it ever so undividedly; it means becoming one spirit with him, what the Apostle makes so plain in the words 'The man who unites himself to the Lord becomes one spirit with him' " (1 Cor 6:17).[60] This unifying action of charity will reach its consummation in eternity when we shall enjoy the Sabbath of Sabbaths, "one same love living in all."[61] Our return to God will be achieved in union with "him the truly ONE, in whom our whole being becomes one . . . one in, through, centered about the ONE: all our knowing and delight, he, the Unique."[62]

59. *Spec.* III, 2, 578b.
61. *Anima*, p. 154.
60. *Spec.* II, 18, 566c.
62. *Spec.* III, 1, 576d.

CHAPTER SEVEN

HOMEWARD JOURNEY

AFTER a penetrating and sympathetic study of medieval spiritual exegesis, Fr de Lubac points out a danger which it did not always succeed in avoiding, the danger, namely, of "losing sight of the social and eschatological aspects,"[1] in the sense that the contemplative, too much taken up, perhaps, with his own spiritual life, may tend to take a microscopic view of hope and forget at times the magnificent vision of the Jerusalem of the Apocalypse. We may ask if the reading of Aelred's works gives one such an impression.

It was shown in the preceding chapter that the social character of returning to God was one of his frequent and favorite themes. It has even been said that, in his teaching, "relationships with other people might well play just as large a part as the purely interior life."[2] If, as we have already shown, the teaching of the Abbot of Rievaulx drew its inspiration completely from Scripture, it is interesting to examine whether his exegesis succeeded in imparting to his teaching a true eschatological orientation. After a brief reminder of the significance history had for these medieval writers who were formed in the school of the Bible, we shall attempt to describe their "pilgrim" attitude of mind and to show that the monastic life has a completely eschatological orientation.

1. H. de Lubac, *Histoire et Esprit. L'intelligence de l'Ecriture d'après Origène*, Paris, 1950, p. 419.
2. L. Bouyer, *The Cistercian Heritage*, p. 126.

Sacred History

A history of the world and the human race in which God did not intervene would have been unthinkable to Christians of the Middle Ages. A history that is not God-centered would have seemed to them an absurd enigma, as absurd as science without method and law would appear to the modern mind. Why? Because to them, saturated in Scripture, history is precisely the action of God in our world, the fulfillment of a divine plan that embraces the entire span of mankind from the creation to the end of the world, a plan that brings salvation to those who know and accept it. The succession of events in history has, therefore, only one meaning: the human race, under God's guidance, is accomplishing a plan of salvation from century to century.[3] God alone knows all the details of this plan. He alone can unveil the meaning of history to us, and this he does through his intervention in these events, through his Word. The Word of God enlightens the past, the present and the future,[4] although in different ways and in such a veiled fashion that their full significance remains hidden.

Such a history is sacred, since it is the history of God. In the mind of God, it is a dispensation designed to lead man out of the "land of wretchedness and darkness," where sin has brought him, and restore the divine likeness in him. It is a long history with various eras[5]—St Augustine handed on to the Middle Ages the traditional account of six ages[6]—and it unfolds in such a way that past events prefigure and pave the way for those of the future. To the Christian, biblical history is thus a mystery in which the "mysteries of Christ

3. See P. Rousset, "La conception de l'histoire à l'époque féodale" in *Mélanges Louis Halphen*, Paris, 1951, pp. 623–33.
4. *S. Ined.*, pp. 31, 52.
5. *S. Ined.*, p. 146.
6. *De Genesi contra Manich.* I, 23, 35–41; P.L. 34, 190–193. See H. de Lubac, *Catholicisme*, 4th ed., 1947, pp. 117–24. C. Rousseau, "Les Pères de l'Eglise et la théologie du temps" in *La Maison-Dieu* 30 (1952) 36–55.

and of the Church" are obscurely presaged and foretold.[7] The sequence of events is unified by the divine purpose governing its continuity: from the world's beginning to its end, it is God's purpose to establish one single society, personified as the Lord's beloved: "From Abel to the holy man who last appears in this world . . . all the saints go to make that one and only Church, referred to in the words: *one is my dove*."[8] Sacred history is but the series of God's overtures of love towards his bride, all unworthy, yet still sought after. From time to time, he sends messengers (Moses, David, Isaiah, Jeremiah) to the one he has chosen, "that holy assembly hand-picked and predestined before the foundation of the world,"[9] in order to intensify the desire for his coming. They foretell the approach of the heavenly Bridegroom, "praise his beauty, boast of his wisdom, extol his power and wealth."[10]

In the series of sermons *De Oneribus* we are constantly presented with the idea of the continuity of God's action throughout three closely connected stages—the history of Israel, the history of Christ, and the history of the Church. The whole of this unfolding history is centered in Christ. He is the Lover of the human race which he found defiled and disabled and enslaved, and yet he united himself to us to bring us happiness.[11] He is the Savior of this sinful race, the Redeemer by whom we return to God. At the center of history stand the passion and resurrection of Christ which won for us our freedom, our Pasch, prefigured by the Jewish Pasch, fulfilled by Christ and consummated by our entrance to the heavenly homeland: "The first Pasch foreshadows Christ's passion; the second is the passion itself; the third shows the effect of the passion in the power of the resurrection."[12]

7. *S. Oner.* I, 365b.　　　　8. *S. Temp.* I, 218b.
9. Cf. Ephes 1:4. *S. Ined.*, p. 40.
10. This is the whole theme of the sermon: *In Epiphania, de tribus generibus nuptiarum, S. Ined.*, pp. 39–47.
11. *S. Ined.*, p. 40.
12. *S. Ined.*, p. 95.

The Christian should not lose sight of this eschatological perspective, for it is the indispensable basis for his hope; it touches the monk in a very special way. Inspired by faith, he no longer pays attention to earthly shadows; the life of this world appears to him merely as a prelude, the first year of his complete history: "Its first year is this present life, the second comes after death, its third follows the resurrection."[13] This is why we must always keep in mind the memory of the paradise we once had, the exile that is now ours, and the heaven we shall one day possess.[14]

Brief Interval

Because the quest for God in monastic life is more absolute than in other states of life, it points the soul towards eschatological realities in a more marked way. Going into solitude is in itself a step that symbolizes, and normally effects, a voluntary estrangement from the things of this world, for the sake of something else that is esteemed preferable. To take such a step is tantamount to regarding the world itself as a desert, and "longing for the true homeland, taking of this world's goods not all the flesh craves, but barely enough to see one through the journey."[15]

The desert is an image that recurs frequently in monastic literature. In this matter, as in so many others, Aelred is distinctly traditional.[16] The desert is the time for seeking God, the mysterious place of our meeting with the Lord, "where the drama of salvation takes place and where the lost paradise is regained spiritually."[17] It is the period of trials and temptations that mark our journey

---

13. *S. Oner.* XXXI, 500c.
14. *S. Ined.,* p. 53.
15. *S. Temp.* V, 244d.
16. See *supra,* pp. 71ff.
17. J. Hild, "L'exode dans la spiritualité chrétienne" in *Vie Spir.* 84 (1951) 250.

towards the land of rest and refreshment.[18] The desert is the march towards the promised land; it is the *interim*,[19] the brief interval, considered in relation to the ultimate life for which it prepares; it is a time of expectancy and quest: "In the time between, Lord, I will seek you."[20] "How ill it goes with us, Lord, for going so far from you. . . . During the present life may my soul grow wings in the nest of your teaching. . . . May it, this side of eternity, love you, the Crucified. . . . Lest forgetfulness cover all with its veil, may my memory be full, in the meantime, of that consoling subject."[21]

This brief interval is a period of trial and purification. Souls destined to be the Lord's throne in heaven must needs be cut and polished, as living stones, on earth.[22] If in heaven a sacrifice of praise rises up to God, the sacrifice of contrition is more often our lot on earth.[23]

Here again we remark the unity and consistency of Aelred's thought. The themes we considered in previous chapters—the return to God, the passage through the desert, the straight way, St Benedict, "our Moses," in community, etc.—are met with again in this context of journeying to the heavenly homeland. It is significant, for example, to note that every sermon for the feast of St Benedict directs our attention to heaven where he is awaiting us: "We are not, of course, bodily present at his side, yet we are,

18. On the spiritual signification of the desert, see: Y. Raguin, *Théologie missionnaire de l'Ancien Testament*, p. 116. St Ambrose, *In Lucam* 4, 7: P.L. 15, 1614. Eucherius, *De laude eremi*: P.L. 50, 701–712. J. Monchanin, "La spiritualité du désert" in *Dieu vivant*, No. 1. On the "flight to the desert" theme in medieval literature, see J. Leclercq, "Ecrits spirituels d'Elmer de Cantorbéry" in *Analecta monastica*, 2nd series, Rome, 1953, pp. 56–57 and M. M. Lebreton, "Les Sermons de Julien, moine de Vézelay" in *Analecta monastica*, 3rd series, 1955, p. 129. For a more modern approach to the spirituality of the desert, see H. Holstein, "Cité ou désert?" in the review *Christus*, no. 1, as well as articles in *Vie Spir.* 88 (1953) 401–15; 89 (1953) 154–72, 369–83, 490–502.

19. On the spiritual significance and importance of *interim*, see F. Chatillon, "Hic, ibi, interim" in *Rev. Asc. Myst.* 25 (1949) 194-99.

20. *Spec.* I, 1, 506a.   21. *Spec.* I, 5, 509d–510a.

22. *S. Ined.*, p. 32.   23. *S. Ined.*, p. 33.

even now, with him through hope and love."[24] His fatherhood, like his mediation, has only one purpose—to lead us on the journey from the land of Egypt to the promised land, through the weariness and afflictions of the desert: "His teaching and care enable us to cross the desert of this present world and reach the promised land referred to by the Prophet in the words: 'This I believe: I shall see the goodness of the Lord in the Land of the Living'" (Ps 26:13).[25]

Like Moses, St Benedict sets up a spiritual tent for the crossing of the desert: the Lord is going to travel with us.[26] The theme of the tabernacle is a favorite one of medieval writers.[27] It is applied to the individual soul, to the monastic life and to the Church. The Church is always a pilgrim Church: "Christ's tabernacle is his Church. Do you follow? Here is God's tabernacle pitched among men. Yes, a tabernacle wherein Christ dwells in his members during their journey; once, however, the promised land is reached, Jerusalem will rise, not as a tent-dwelling, but as a city."[28] Towards this heavenly city a monk directs all his yearning: "We are, all of us, journeying to one same city; our one desire is to be enrolled among its citizens."[29] The same desire fills the whole Church: "Her name is Jerusalem not because she has the clear sight the angels have of peace, but because, through faith, good deeds and burning love, she goes towards him, who is our peace, Jesus Christ our Lord."[30]

These quotations prove, therefore, that Aelred's teaching is in no way affected by any microscopic view of hope. He never ceases to put before his monks the image of the city that is to come: "This is

24. *S. Temp.* VI, 245a.
25. *S. Temp.* VII, 247d–248a.   26. *Ibid.*, 248b.
27. See Adam Scot, *De tripartito tabernaculo*, P.L. 198, 609–792 (Cf. M.D. Chenu, "Théologie symbolique et exégèse scolastique aux XIIᵉ et XIIIᵉ siècles" in *Mélanges J. de Ghellinck*, t. II, pp. 512–13). Peter of Celle, *De tabernaculo Moysi*, P.L. 202, 1047–1084 (Cf. J. Leclercq, *La spiritualité de Pierre de Celle*, pp. 34–36). Peter of Poitiers, *Tractatus super tabernaculum Moysi*: ed. Ph. S. Moore and J. Corbett, Notre Dame, Indiana, 1938.
28. *S. Ined.*, p. 157.   29. *S. Temp.* II, 220d.
30. *S. Temp.* X, 265d

that city that is one day to be the heavenly city we look for, our mother. . . . Built amidst the inviolate hills, dearer to the Lord than any other home in Jacob; its streets pure gold. . . . City that has no need of sun or moon to show in it; the glory of God shines there."[31]

Assuredly Aelred's perspective is eschatological; all these quotations and scriptural images fit into the magnificent setting of the Apocalypse. The kingdom that is described for us here in its perfect and definitive fulfillment already exists on earth in the hearts of the faithful. Aelred describes it in the words of St Paul: this kingdom of God is "rightness of heart, finding our peace and joy in the Holy Spirit" (Rom 14:17). After it will come another that cannot be described: "things no eye has seen, no ear has heard, no human heart conceived" (1 Cor 2:9).[32] St Benedict has pointed out to his monks a direct and sure way to reach this kingdom, namely, his Rule: "If we keep this law, we shall inherit the kingdom of Heaven."[33] In the course of this journey it is the abbot's duty to break the bread needed by the pilgrims for their journey: "It is for you to ask us bread, for us to break it for you. It is our duty to break the bread God destines for your journey through this world, that you may, with angels for your company, enjoy the heavenly, unbroken bread stored up for you in your homeland. The bread for your journey is the mystery of Christ's incarnation and the truth of his teaching. . . . The bread of the homeland . . . is the face-to-face vision of God."[34]

Angelic Life

When a Christian has set his heart on, and seeks, the things of eternity, he is inclined to make little of passing things: "Yes, all that passes, all that sometime ceases, is only momentary. For this reason,

---

31. *S. Ined.*, p. 174. 32. *S. Temp.* XV, 298a–b.
33. *S. Temp.* V, 240c. 34. *S. Temp.* IV, 234b.

the Holy Spirit would have us fix our desire on what is eternal and not make much of what is gone with time."[35] This is the way the saints passed through this life, led by the Spirit, having no permanent dwelling on earth: "Carried about like so many tents by the Holy Spirit, the saints journey through this world. Though they, like tents, may be set up at the moment in Babylon, it is not their lasting city; the city they look for is that which one day will be in heaven."[36] One consequence of such a view of things is an evaluation of this present life that is considerably different from the modern theological view of earthly things. The present life is judged in comparison with eternal life, and the contrast that results leaves us with a dismal enough picture of the former: "Our lives in this world are a tissue of fear, of toil, of suffering; not for us the sight of God, the joys of paradise, the food of heaven."[37] "This life means suffering, that rest; danger here makes way for safety there; present poverty yields to plenty then; grief now, but gladness hereafter; here hunger and thirst, there full contentment."[38]

Why then do we not grasp the true meaning of life and desire to pass, like St Benedict, "from earth to heaven, from prison to palace, from death to life, from wretchedness to glory"?[39] Our present life ought to be totally directed to eternal life, for there is, in fact, a close connection between the two: "Comfort will be ours in the life to come in proportion to what we suffer in Christ's service at present."[40]

This might appear to be a pessimistic outlook, and, in a certain sense, it is, in so far as it bears on the things that pass. But it would, perhaps, be more correct to say that this eschatological view of life lends enchantment to the desert trek, inasmuch as it tends to transform it into an anticipation of eternal life. Even on earth monks practice the "angelic life." The spiritual city, which is the monastery, should be peopled with "angelic" citizens: "In this city we become

35. *S. Oner.* XIII, 416a.
36. *Ibid.,* 414b.
37. *Inst.* 11, p. 116.
38. *S. Temp.* XXIII, 341c.
39. *S. Temp.* VI, 245b.
40. *S. Temp.* XIII, 284d; XXIII, 341b.

citizens . . . of the angels' city. Our observances prove us fellow citizens of the angels."[41]

This does not mean that monks are detached from their bodies—experience proves that they are no angels in this sense[42]—nor that they live in angelic purity—they sin at least seven times a day—but it means that their lives are totally orientated towards heaven, where the vision and possession of God are to be found. They imitate the angels by being taken up with God and his praise.[43] Destined to form, with the angels, one single throne for the Lord, they are, so to speak, substitute angels.[44] The angels are, moreover, always close to those who on earth endeavor to imitate their life: "They are among those chanting psalms, encourage those at prayer, are at the side of those who read and meditate."[45] And in a community of monks, vowed to the service of God, the splendor of the angelic virtues of chastity, charity, humility, obedience and harmonious unity shines forth.[46]

The liturgy promotes this eschatological thrust: it leads us to anticipate and desire the heavenly liturgy. The chants, the hymns, the lights we use are so many symbols of the everlasting festivities: "The psalms are a symbol of the everlasting jubilee that follows from the indescribable joy the saints have in God. The hymns represent the praise past all telling they ceaselessly offer to God. . . . The many lamps are a reminder of the eternal light in which the saints have their dwelling."[47] Each liturgical act recalls to us God's blessings, reanimates our hope and makes us yearn for our ultimate happiness, "that through reflecting on it our longing and love for it grow ever greater."[48]

In this respect, Lent is in particular a great sacrament, since it recalls to us the very meaning of our destiny. It moves the

41. S. *Temp.* II, 221c.

42. See *supra*, pp. 74–75.

43. See J. Leclercq, *La vie parfaite*, pp. 21–24.

44. S. *Ined.*, pp. 32 and 38.

45. S. *Oner.* V, 318d.

46. S. *Temp.* XXIII, 347c.

47. S. *Temp.* XXII, 336c.

48. S. *Temp.* XXIII, 340c.

Christian to compunction,[49] lamenting his wretchedness and longing for the peace of heaven. He remembers the paradise he has lost, and thinks of the destitution that is now his lot. The present life appears to him as worthless and wearisome, but the thought of the life to come adds fuel to his desire.[50] Desire, desire of God, desire of heaven is the predominant disposition of the soul that seeks the good things to come:[51] "Event so deserving of desire and welcome! Ever the object of every saint's every-day prayer."[52] The Advent liturgy[53] breathes into the Christian soul a longing for the glorious coming of Christ such as the holy men of the Old Law had for his bodily coming.[54] This desire for the heavenly city[55] finds frequent expression in Aelred's works, an impetuous desire that makes the soul soar swiftly to the heights: "hope, whereby heaven is preferred to earth, eternity to time, God to man; through which we are already saved and sit as kings with Christ on high. Despair, however, destroys it when . . . the soul stoops to what is unworthy and engages all its affection, not on heavenly, but on earthly objects, looking for nothing else, hoping for naught besides."[56]

Souls thus given to contemplating the things of eternity experience at certain moments the truth of St Paul's words: "We find our true home in heaven" (Phil 3:20).[57] Aelred has expressed very

49. *Inst.* 11, p. 186; see the two sermons for Lent, *S. Ined.*, pp. 52–62.

50. *S. Ined.*, p. 53.

51. Equally characteristic is the influence of St Gregory on medieval monastic spirituality on this point. See J. Leclercq in *Analecta monastica*, 1st series, p. 78: "This desire, the desire for God . . . is, so to speak, the dynamic principle of the whole interior life. The monks of the Middle Ages, who had received this doctrine of supreme importance from St Gregory, passed it on in their many and varied writings."

52. *S. Ined.*, p. 32.

53. See sermons *De Adventu, S. Temp.* I, 209–220. *S. Ined.*, pp. 31–37. To these may be added : P.L. 184, 817–829; and also *S. Temp.* X, 264–271, which, though entitled *In ramis palmarum*, is actually a sermon for Advent.

54. *S. Temp.* I, 210a.

55. *S. Temp.* XIII, 290a. *S. Temp.* II, 221d. *S. Temp.* III, 228d.

56. *S. Oner.* XXI, 450a.

57. See *S. Temp.* VII, 250b.

beautifully what it means to find our true home in heaven: con-
templatives "with eyes lifted to heaven . . . make little of all that
passes and is of earth, count it no better than so much smoke and
shadow; they are carried away not only by burning love of (*per
excessum mentis*[58]) but by ceaseless longing for heaven's joys; their
gaze is so fixed on God in heaven that they not only have their fill
of delight divine, they overflow with heavenly gladness. And this is
why their chanting in choir is so fervent, their prayer so pure; why,
often, in the ardor and power of the Holy Spirit, their mind is
swept away and comes so close to what is heavenly and eternal that
they are tempted to think themselves no longer mortal."[59]

Consequently death no longer appears as destruction, but rather
as the end of wayfaring and the entry into the true life so earnestly
desired by the soul. During the course of its journey the soul has
many times realized that death, in some form, was the inevitable
prelude to entrance into the various spiritual sanctuaries; there had
always to be a gradually greater shedding of the burdens and
impurities of the flesh. Its ascent to God was marked by these
separations of "body" and soul: "the separation [of soul and body]
can come about in three ways: by love, by rapture, by death."[60] To
the soul that has long yearned for beatitude, the supreme separation,
death, should hold no terrors: "Here is something greater than all
the pleasures, honors and wealth of the world . . . that when death
approaches the natural dread it inspires is mastered by faith, made
bearable by hope, routed by peace of conscience."[61] Happy the
soul who, "so pure in conscience, so sure in hope," sees in death
"the foretaste of the freedom of beatitude," "the beginning of what
lies in the future, the end of what now is."[62]

---

58. See *infra,* note 60.   59. *S. Ined.,* p. 174.
    60. *S. Ined.,* p. 128. The separation denoted by *affectus* is the passage from
affectus carnalis et corporalis to *affectus spiritualis.* The *excessus* here designates a
mystical experience. The *transitus* coincides with bodily death.
    61. *Inst.,* 33, p. 213.
    62. *Ibid.*

We return to God through Christ.[63] But Christ reigns now in heaven. Already incorporated in him as members of the body of which he is the head, our aim must be to unite ourselves ever more closely with his heavenly life: "This should be our only concern, to cling to him with all our heart, soul, strength; keeping ever in mind that he is our Head. Yes, he is the whole meaning of our lives. It is for us to live as becomes the followers of so great a Leader. We must set our hearts, not here where our bodies are, but on heaven . . . making it our earnest prayer to the Father Almighty . . . that our whole affection be fixed where our nature, in Jesus Christ, lives and rules at his side."[64]

Aelred encourages his sister to meditate often on the glory and joy awaiting us all in the kingdom of heaven. Christ then will have united in himself all the images of God, made anew in his likeness and united in his life; "each and every member joined and bound in closest love, in everlasting bliss, to its Head."[65] In the company of the angels, we shall take part in the triumphant procession that will mark the close of the economy of salvation, the restoration of the human race and its return once and for all to the Father.[66] The soul will then be in peace, for it will have found its beatitude. God will give himself to each one "to the extent of each one's fitness,"[67] and the Blessed Trinity will be the happiness of all: "The Father will be seen in the Son, the Son in the Father, the Holy Spirit in each of the others."[68] The image will have attained the place of its rest. And yet, the desire for deeper knowledge and love of him, whose perfect reflection it will be at last, will be so strong that no satiety will diminish it, and of such a kind that it will be no bar to the fullness of happiness:[69] "That vision will be ours forever, and ever will we go on desiring it."[70]

63. See part I, chapter I, section *Through Christ*.
64. *S. Temp.* XIII, 290a.   65. *S. Ined.*, p. 42.   66. *Inst.* 33, p. 215.
67. *Ibid.*, p. 216.   68. *Ibid.*
69. *Inst.* p. 216: *tanta desiderii vehemencia ut nec satietas desiderium minuat nec desiderium satietatem impediat.*   70. *S. Ined.*, p. 36.

CONCLUSION

ARRANGING the material furnished by an analysis of his writings, and allowing him to speak for himself, we have made a general survey of Aelred's theology. We have shown how this theology had a profound influence upon his concept of the monastic life. It remains now to synthesize the results of our investigation, and, after merely touching on the problem of his sources, we shall attempt to indicate the extent of his originality.

Results of the Analysis

This concrete exposition of, and collection of quotations from, the teaching of Aelred of Rievaulx (which may perhaps appear too much like a mosaic), seems to call for a more systematic presentation to round it off. We do not intend simply to summarize what we have discovered in the course of this study. To avoid producing an arid inventory, we shall group these conclusions under several main headings.

1. Method: Aelred teaches by means of provocative themes

He does not establish theses nor expound a system. His is no abstract teaching; rather it is frequently the testimony of his own

N

experience to express which he uses images and symbols.[1] Consequently, if we are to deduce the main lines of his doctrine, we have first to discover and list his themes in their myriad variety, and then arrange them, not however in strict scholastic fashion, underlining their inter–relationship and mutual influence.

2. *Unity of doctrine*

An examination of his works reveals a doctrinal unity. But to guard against misconception, we should point out that a synthesis is not elaborated in the way we understand a synthesis today. Nowhere in his works will we find a complete and methodic presentation of it. Therefore we have had to reconstruct and arrange such a synthesis, something which appears to be required by his whole work.

3. *Doctrinal synthesis—history of salvation*

It is impossible to understand monastic writers like Aelred, or have any relish for their works, if we do not grasp their spiritual *Weltanschauung*, which, like the *Gnosis* of the Fathers, is a general perspective of the divine economy of redemption and restoration. Aelred's attention is focused on this mystery, both in its objective and historical reality and in its subjective and individual fulfillment. From the first point of view, sacred history is essentially Christocentric—Christ is its center and climax—and ecclesiological—the Church is seen as the assembly of all the righteous from Abel to the last just man on earth. From the latter point of view, sacred history is the story of the withdrawal from God of his created image and

1. Expression by means of images and symbols had a special importance in the theology of the monks of the Middle Ages. See Z. Alszeghy, "Contributi alla teologia bernardiana" in *Gregorianum* 38 (1957) 338.

of its return, by way of charity, to him: hence the importance of the treatises *On the Soul* and the *Mirror of Charity*, both owing their inspiration to St Augustine.

4. Scripture: the soul of his whole teaching

Aelred thinks, speaks, prays and judges with the Bible. From it his doctrine draws its food and its sweetness. The Word of God is the soul of his theology, the Bible his textbook of monastic formation. There is no need to emphasize this point again; it is sufficient to summarize it by saying that for him Scripture is the doctrinal source *par excellence*, a spiritual mirror for scrutinizing his thoughts and actions,[2] the source of the soul's reformation, "the source of re-education,"[3] and one of the privileged meeting-places with God by way of *lectio divina*.

5. Close connection between his monastic ideal and his doctrine

Monastic life, as described by Aelred, is first and foremost the Christian life.[4] In line with the history of salvation it has but one aim: to be a more sure way of returning to God. It is a journey, a progress, a march, a pilgrimage; hence its dynamic character and its eschatological orientation. His turn of speech is frequently biblical (see chapter 3).

2. *Spec.* II, 14, 559c. *S. Ined.*, p. 52.
3. *S. Oner.* I, 363d. Cf. *Spec.* I, 5, 509b.
4. This is a characteristic of St Gregory's teaching too. There is such a thing as a monastic doctrine: cf. O. Porcel, *La doctrina monastica de San Gregorio magno y la Regula monachorum*, Madrid, 1950. And yet, as Dom R. Gillet remarks, in *Grégoire le Grand, Morales sur Job* (Coll. *Sources chrétiennes*), in his homilies "which are primarily monastic conferences" (p. 10), he has constantly in view "the spiritual plenitude which should be that of every true Christian" (p. 102).

o

6. *Richness and variety in unity*

In this study of Aelred's works, we advanced from the simple to the multiple, in the sense that the questions examined became progressively more complex. The three salient features studied in Part 3 should never, in fact, be viewed in isolation, nor separated from the other various themes of Aelred's doctrine. These themes cannot properly be understood except in their composite whole and their mutual relationship. The *experience* theme, for example, involves the study of man (the experiences of withdrawal from God, sin, wretchedness etc., experience of love and friendship), monastic life (experience of flight from the world, the hardships of the desert, etc.), the reading of Scripture, etc. Furthermore every Christian experience takes place in the Church, it is a community experience. The *community* theme, in its turn, is based on the nature of man, on the divine plan of salvation and on the cenobitic form of monastic life. The *eschatological* theme, finally, is closely related to the other themes—image, Scripture, the Church, monasticism. It will be seen, therefore, how important it is always to keep the whole picture in mind. In a study such as this we must examine each of these elements separately, but there is constant need to be on our guard against cutting up the doctrine piecemeal, a doctrine that is integral because it is living.

Sources of Aelred's Doctrine

The claim to understand an author's doctrine without having referred to the sources from which he drew it, is a questionable one. No man is an island. But it is not so obvious that the first problem to be dealt with when studying any doctrine is this investigation of sources.[5] It would appear more logical first to examine the work

5. So experienced a historian as M.H.I. Marrou is of the same opinion: "It seems to us that our first task is to rediscover, to grasp anew and to understand

itself, deduce its main features, bring out its overall unity. It will then be possible and instructive to distinguish, by way of comparison, what is original from what is not. Such a task is beyond the scope of this work and would supply the material for a book that would take up where this one ends.

Always a difficult investigation, the task is particularly so in the case of a medieval monastic writer whose aim was to remain faithful to tradition, who expressed himself in biblical terms, who considered the heritage of the Fathers as his own and quoted them without bothering about references. All of which is not the mark of intellectual slavishness, but of a mind that was very much alive. The themes were borrowed, but the experience was original and authentic. It is supremely important to remember this, if we are to form a just estimate of these writers. It would be unfair to draw up a minute list of their citations and then accuse them of plagiarism. The truth is not so simple as that; Aelred's originality, as we shall see, is to be sought less in the fundamental ideas, which after all are common property, than in the sincerity of his expression of them, in the truth and relative newness of his testimony, and in the coherence of his doctrinal synthesis. Here we desire only to give some clear notions that will help to situate Aelred's doctrine in the history of religious thought, no more than a few indications that may serve as a basis for further study.

Aelred was a monk of the Middle Ages. His chief source, therefore, was Sacred Scripture,[6] the food of his intellectual and spiritual

---

some particular doctrine, in its inner structure, its consistency, its extent and its value. The thought of an author or a school is a historical object in itself, possessing its own essence and meriting consideration. We ought not be in too much of a hurry to reduce it to a combination of borrowed or inherited elements. The *Quellenforschung* becomes lawful and has meaning only on condition that it is preceded by this primary work of understanding" (Introduction to the Collection *Patristica Sorbonensia*, in Michael Spanneut, *Le Stoïcisme des Pères de l'Eglise*, Paris, 1957, p. 9).

6. See *supra*, p. 86.

life. This food he received in *lectio divina* and in the liturgy.[7] His knowledge of Scripture was deepened by the reading of the Fathers,[8] so much so that his theological method is akin to the patristic *gnosis*.[9]

St Augustine not only provided Aelred with his principal themes, but frequently influenced his turn of thought and phrase as well. Aelred had a personal devotion to him; he felt they were kindred souls. Even a superficial acquaintance with his works makes this kinship apparent. Aelred belonged to the great Augustinian movement that had such a profound influence on medieval thought. Constant reading of the writings of the great Doctor made him familiar with his doctrine. In the single treatise *On the Soul*, C. H. Talbot has noted 180 points of affinity between Aelred's and Augustine's doctrine. To mention only a few of the themes adopted by Aelred: love, beatitude, charity, form, memory, wretchedness, withdrawal from God, rest, order, etc.

Frequently, too, there are terms, images and symbols drawn from St Gregory to be found in Aelred's works, such as compunction, conversion, desire, peace, visitation, and the half-hour of the Apocalypse applied to contemplation.

While it is relatively easy to discover in Aelred traces of Scotus Erigenus, Isidore of Seville, Raban Maurus and the Venerable Bede,[10] it is more difficult to determine precisely what he owed to the Greek Fathers. The general influence of Origen on his exegesis

---

7. Cf. *supra*, pp. 122ff. Of some 1500 scriptural quotations noted in Aelred's sermons and treatises, 714 are taken from the four Gospels, 608 from the Psalms, 362 from the Epistles to the Romans and the Corinthians. These figures would suggest that the *milieu de vie* in which Aelred became familiar with these sacred texts is the liturgy. The Song of Songs, much loved by the twelfth-century monks, is quoted 81 times.

8. See *supra*, pp. 97ff.

9. *Ibid.*, pp. 87 and 162.

10. For St Augustine's influence upon Aelred and for his other patristic sources, see P. Courcelle, "Ailred de Rievaulx à l'école des Confessions" in *Revue des Etudes augustiniennes* 111–12 (1957) 163–74; and C. H. Talbot, *Ailred of Rievaulx, de Anima*, introduction, pp. 51–54.

is beyond question. It is equally certain that the library of Rievaulx, as its catalogue records, possessed, besides Origen's writings, works of St Basil, St Gregory Nazianzen and St John Chrysostom. But to what extent Aelred himself read them, it is difficult to know.

Besides the Fathers, we may also include some of Aelred's contemporaries among his sources. A similarity between his theology and that of the School of Laon has been noted, but to prove it beyond question, more light has still to be shed on the doctrine of Master Anselm. In a different field, we find echoes of prayers by St Anselm and John of Fecamp, which prove that the Abbot of Rievaulx was acquainted with the works of these writers.

For the monks of the Middle Ages there is another source, the importance of which, perhaps, is not sufficiently emphasized, and that is oral tradition.[11] From century to century it transmitted unbroken a particular genre of spirituality in monastic circles. We have to take this factor into account and remember that Aelred's doctrine finds its setting in the Cistercian Order of the twelfth century, in which the influence of St Bernard was so marked. Aelred inevitably came under this influence, for the founders of Rievaulx, the very monks who formed him to the monastic life, came from Clairvaux and were familiar with Bernard's teaching. They had brought with them his manuscripts, and so from his novitiate Aelred was imbued with the doctrine expounded in the treatises *On the Degrees of Humility, On Loving God, On Grace and Free Will,* etc. It is impossible to deny the importance of this influence.

Finally Aelred was a twelfth-century humanist, which is one of the most interesting aspects of his character. It likewise sheds light on the problem of his sources. Cicero was a favorite of his, especially when he was young, and is the immediate source of his treatise *On Spiritual Friendship.*[12]

11. Cf. Z. Alszeghy, *Gregorianum* 38 (1957) 334.
12. Cf. J. Dubois, *Aelred de Rievaulx, L'amitié spirituelle,* Introduction, pp. xlviii and following.

Aelred's Originality

Aelred was able to take in the elements he received from Scripture, the liturgy, the Fathers and monastic tradition and assimilate them in a way that was peculiarly his own. He rethought them, tested them, experienced them for himself, and this is precisely what constitutes the originality of his teaching, and likewise its charm, for Aelred was no mediocre person. The stamp Aelred left on his works was the product of his own personality, his humanistic culture and the healthy realism of his spirituality.

As we have said above,[13] his characteristic trait seems to be an affective disposition, a blend of courtesy, gentleness of manner and a goodness that touched on tenderness. Aelred was remembered by the monks of his time as the personification of the "loving-kindness of monks."[14] But his affective nature was under perfect control and was always thoughtful of others. He had opposition to endure, and was a target for criticism from monks actuated by bitter zeal.[15] Yet always he preserved an amazing patience with, and compassion for, the weaknesses of others,[16] and he retained not the least trace of spitefulness towards those who hurt him. If a false friend could never again be admitted to intimacy with him, "never did he withdraw his affection from him, grudge him help or refuse advice."[17] He was grieved when he saw one of his sons going astray.[18] It is hardly necessary to add that Aelred, warm-hearted and full of affection though he was, was in no way effeminate. Proof of this can be found in the quality of his leadership of a great

13. See *supra*, p. 61ff.

14. Nicolas of Clairvaux, P.L. 195, 207–208.

15. *Vita*, p. 33. See F. M. Powicke, Introduction to the *Vita*, pp. xxx and lxv.

16. Jocelin of Furness, *Vita S.Waldeni: Acta Sanctorum*, 3a Augusti, t. I, ed. Palme: 258c-d: *Erat nihilominus supra omnes coaetaneos suos ecclesiae praelator mansuetus et patiens, et infirmitatibus corporum et morum aliorum valde compatiens.*

17. *Am.* III, 687a, p. 131.　　　　　　18. *S. Temp.* XXIII, 343a.

abbey, where not all the monks were courteous and easy to get on with,[19] his practical love of austere observances and his devotion to the cross of Christ which he preached by word[20] and example.[21]

There is a more curious, and for us a more surprising, side to Aelred's character. This medieval monk, this teacher of monks, was a *humanist* of no indifferent calibre, but one who was thoroughly typical of the culture of his time. An English historian, as discriminating as he is scholarly, Professor David Knowles states that at Rievaulx, the Rievaulx of Aelred, he discovered "the quintessence of the humanism of the twelfth century."[22] By this he means that he found, harmoniously blended in the person and writings of Aelred, these three characteristic traits: "first, a wide literary culture; next, a great and what in the realm of religious sentiment would be called a personal devotion to certain figures of the ancient world; and finally a high value set upon the individual, personal emotions, and upon the sharing of experiences and opinions within a small circle of friends."[23] Aelred did, in fact, possess a literary culture, less obvious, no doubt, than in other writers, but still quite apparent in his works. He showed a special devotion, at least in his youth, for Cicero, whose treatise on friendship he christianized, and, above all, for St Augustine to whom he looked as "a guide in his own pilgrimage."[24] His works and his life amply bear witness to his desire for expressing his personal emotions and for intimate conversations with his friends.[25] By reason of these humanistic traits, the good Aelred finds himself in rather surprising company, that of Abelard and Héloïse, two other figures of the twelfth century, whose careers were more stormy than his. Professor Knowles

---

19. See, for example, the incident related in the *Epistola ad Mauricium*, appended to the *Vita*, p. 79.

20. *S. Temp.* IX, 263c-d.

21. *Vita*, pp. 54-55.

22. "The Humanism of the Twelfth Century" in *Studies* 30 (1941) 43-58. It is worth reading the whole of this interesting article.

23. *Ibid.*, p. 46.   24. *Ibid.*, p. 52.

25. *Vita*, p. 40.

remarks that Aelred's gifts of mind and soul were in some ways unique.[26]

The originality of Aelred's monastic teaching lies also in the sound and balanced realism that underlies the entire formation he gave his monks. This may, perhaps, have been due to his Anglo-Saxon temperament, but even more it should be ascribed to the spirit of supernatural wisdom that made Aelred take heed of the particular circumstances and capacities of men as they actually are. He did not forget that monks have bodies and that it is imprudent to tax them beyond their powers;[27] that their souls are endowed with the power to love, those inclinations it is impossible to deny and wise to turn to account.[28] At the same time, he evinced, as a spiritual guide, an understanding of God and his ways. He showed the soul confused by the ups and downs of its spiritual life, that the Lord "comes . . . withdraws . . . returns . . . and hides himself."[29] And if he required his monks to practice asceticism manfully, he did not fail to take into consideration the part played by God.[30] His natural flair for psychology coupled with the discretion of his Benedictine training made him realize by experience that no two souls are alike, and that an abbot must adapt himself to the varying situations arising from circumstances and diverse personalities: "This person awaits the encouragement his spiritual father alone can grant him . . .; that other, with no outlet for the venom in his heart, complains internally of his superior . . .; another, the victim of tepidity, looks in vain for someone to help him."[31] Some men are won by a gracious exterior, who would be completely discouraged and disturbed in soul by an outer severity.[32] How is one to deal with these? Try to understand them and help them to direct their emotions to the

---

26. *Art. cit.* p. 53.
27. *Spec.* III, 23, 596c: *ne metas corporeae possibilitatis excedat.*
28. *Spec.* III, 25, 598.
29. *S. Temp.* XXV, 355d–356b.
30. *S. Oner.* V, 383d. *S. Oner.* XXIX, 489b. *S. Ined.*, p. 142.
31. *S. Oner.* XXVIII, 485c. *Jesu*, P.L. 184, 868c.
32. *Spec.* III, 19, 593–594.

service of true charity. Again Aelred teaches us that it is indiscreet, and therefore imprudent, to set all souls aiming at full-time contemplation, or shepherd all into an exclusively active life of occupations and charges in the monastery. There is a time for everything, and it is the part of wisdom to wed, under obedience, the active life with the contemplative:[33] "We must overcome idleness by varying our exercises; keep ourselves steady by changing our occupations."[34]

The varied character of Aelred's teaching fits him to be an understanding spiritual guide for monks. He does not attempt to minimize the efforts demanded of them, but the renunciation he preaches has nothing in common with an unnatural radicalism. On the contary, the road pointed out by him and the atmosphere created by him tended to develop an individual's personality to the full.[35] In the school of this master, a monk willingly consents, step by step, to all the necessary self-denial, and by means of these sufferings of the desert, he opens up more and more to friendship with God and men.

The theologian who is interested in the study and comparison of "the various forms in which the same truths of faith are rendered intelligible in different ages"[36] will not miss the significance and interest of this study of Aelred. The basic doctrine remains the same, since it has come from on high, but its formulation varies and its speculative elaboration develops. St Augustine's theological method is not that of Suarez, nor of Origen or St Thomas, and yet all of them are theologians. Can we claim that Aelred is a typical representative of what has been called monastic theology? Before we can answer this question, we should need to reach an agreement on

33. *S. Temp.* XVII, 306.

34. *Inst.*, p. 184.

35. L. Bouyer, *The Cistercian Heritage*, p. 126: "(Aelred's) Christian and monastic ideal found expression in the form of a development of the human personality."

36. Z. Alszeghy, "Contributi alla teologia bernardiana" in *Gregorianum* 38 (1957) 340.

what exactly is meant by monastic theology. While some admit
there is such a theology and adduce adequate grounds for it,[37] others
are cautious about accepting it.

Any definition of monastic theology that would set it in opposition to scholastic theology would hardly fail to cause annoyance.
To push the distinction to the extent of suggesting that the former
is totally independent of the latter is perilous: theology is catholic
or it is not theology at all, and hence there is only one theology in
the Church.[38] On the other hand, to regard monastic theology as a
superseded historical fact, nothing more than a prelude to the
theology of the thirteenth century, would be inaccurate and unjust.
Attempting to clarify what is the distinctive mark of this theology,
it may be affirmed that it is closely connected with the notion of
Christian experience.[39] But the difficulty still remains, for, although
J. Mouroux has made a penetrating analysis of this experience,[40] the
concept of it which he finally presents appears so complicated that
we cannot help sharing the doubt of some theologians as to its
applicability to medieval writers.[41]

How then are we to set about gaining some idea of monastic
theology? The best way appears to be to adopt the analytic de-
scriptive method, that is, try to get inside the mentality of the
medieval monks, to understand their thought from the inside, and
then using their own terminology, describe its various intellectual
and affective developments. This is what we have attempted to do

37. Dom J. Leclercq in *The Love of Learning and the Desire for God* has expounded, with all the necessary nuances, the characteristics of this theology
as he, a historian, has discovered them in medieval monastic literature.

38. See E. Gilson, "La Cité de Dieu de Saint Bernard ou la Théologie
catholique est une" in *Saint Bernard, homme de l'Eglise*, La Pierre-qui-Vire,
1953, pp. 101–15.

39. J. Leclercq, *Saint Bernard Théologien*, p. 15: monastic theology "is based
on the 'Christian experience' outlined for us by M. Mouroux. . ."

40. J. Mouroux, *The Christian Experience. An Introduction to a Theology*,
trans. G. Lamb, London, 1955.

41. Z. Alszeghy, *art. cit.*, p. 332.

in this book. It would be idle to pretend that we have been completely successful; the task is a delicate one. However such a study is, in itself, of great interest.

It is wrong to describe the theology of the monks as something in opposition to the theology of the scholastics; the truth is that they are two aspects of the one sacred doctrine: "These two ways of seeking to understand the Christian revelation are lawful and traditional. They are two complementary methods of theological investigation. . . . Each has its advantages and its dangers. Far from being mutually exclusive, they ought to complement and verify each other."[42] The richness of these two theological methods ought to stimulate the curiosity and the minds of theologians. The student for the priesthood, who applies himself to the scholastic method for several years, should feel that contact with these spiritual writers of the Middle Ages is a necessary complement to his theological training.[43] There he will learn to relish another form of religious thought, less abstract in its expression, more synthetic in its general perspective of the mystery of salvation,[44] more practical[45] in the sense that it is more directly aimed at life, and because of this we would say more exacting. It presupposes in the subject purification, personal commitment, a keener sense of mystery—in a word, a more real identity between a man's thinking and his way of living.

By his *Mirror of Charity*, his *On Spiritual Friendship* and his personal warmth of affection, the Abbot of Rievaulx reminds us that the Word of the living God should make us theologians who have that special gift of clear-sightedness which is given to the pure of soul and fervent of heart. In his own way, this twelfth-century Cistercian directs the attention of twentieth-century clerics to the

42. J. Leclercq, *Saint Bernard Théologien*, p. 15.

43. Z. Alszeghy, *art. cit.*, p. 340.

44. A characteristic of the *gnosis* of the Fathers; the monastic writers of the Middle Ages retained the same general perspective of the plan of salvation. See G. Vagaggini, *La natura della sintesi origeniana e l'ortodossia e l'eterodossia della dogmatica di Origene: La Scuola cattolica*, 1954, pp. 190ff.

45. J. Leclercq, *op. cit.*, p. 15.

fact that the theologian who is no more than a professor is in a very bad way.[46] Aelred too could exclaim: "Woe upon the sterile knowledge that does not lead to love." How could such a theology be regarded as out-of-date? On the contrary, it is very relevant for the present day, since it expresses, as does the monastic life itself, truths of lasting value for the Church and for mankind.[47] Modern theologians are interested in these values. Their contact with the writers of old poses many questions. We cannot examine these here, but the problem awaits a solution. It is our sincere hope that we may have helped the reader to a clearer understanding of the reality and interest of this problem for modern theology.

46. M. D. Chenu, "Culture et théologie à Jumièges après l'ère féodale" in *Jumièges*, t. II, p. 781.
47. *Ibid.*

ANALYTIC INDEX

Affectus : complexity and richness of this concept 29; characteristic qualities of the love-*affectus* 30; its importance in Aelred's doctrine 30, 117, 121; man's attitude towards God is basically a matter of *affectus* 41, 42; inseparable from spiritual knowledge and experience 118, 121.

Beatitude: desire for happiness is indestructible 16, 18, 32; man's happiness consists in union with God 32, 33, 41, 51–52; this union is achieved chiefly by love 31, 32; beatitude coincides with the image's perfect restoration 133–134; desire continues in beatitude 124–125, 160.

Benedict, Saint: Benedict is seen by Aelred in a biblical setting: he is our Moses 73, 106–108; his role of fatherhood in our regard 106–108; he makes us disciples of the Fathers 98; eulogy of his Rule 105; he makes way for Jesus to lead us into the promised land (contemplation) 77; in returning to God he is our model 106; eschatological aspect of all Aelred's sermons on St Benedict 153.

Charity: see *love* and *cupidity*. Aelred makes a clear distinction between charity and cupidity: charity is the right use of love while cupidity is the wrong use of love. Hence the opposition between them 43. Charity is God's sabbath 35; it is the reason for creation 35. In the case of man charity consists in the union of the human will with the divine 38, 128; its criterion is not *affectus* 128. Monastic life is based on charity 67–68; spiritual friendship is charity, a most sacred kind of charity 36; spiritual experience nourishes charity 132; charity sums up all perfection 52; the goal of the return to God is unity in charity 147.

Choice: love's first step: a choice guided by reason 30.

Christ: the necessary mediator for the return to God 19–20; redeemer and peacemaker 19; restorer of the image 20; no spiritual friendship can exist without Christ 21, 38; Jesus replaces St Benedict for the entry into the promised land 77; liturgical feasts, memorials of Christ 102; eschatological aspect of our union with the risen Christ 22, 160; united with the angels we shall form one throne for the Lord 157.

Church: biblical ecclesiology: the people of God on the march 135–136, 150; the Bride of Christ 137, 151; the monastery is a church, that is, a community of salvation 68, 135–138; the Church is one 151.

Cupidity: contrary to charity 42; cause of the withdrawal from God

and of wretchedness 11–12, 40;
is the antithesis of charity 43;
cupidity cannot be rectified, it
must be destroyed 43; Aelred
stresses the evil consequences of
cupidity, even in the cloister 46,
74–75, 82–83, 145; the choice—
cupidity or friendship 40–52.

Discretion: one of the characteristics
of Aelred's personality and teaching 62–63; 170–171.

Eruditio: for the distinction between
eruditio and *disciplina* see p. 85,
note 1. *Euriditio* means "reformation," the form being wisdom 80. It is both instruction and
incentive in the school of Christ
80, 115; it involves faith, hope and
charity 80, 132. It is primarily a
regulating of charity 82, 111–112.
Scripture is the source of *eruditio*
80, 163.

Experience: one of the characteristic
features of Aelred's teaching 120–
121; a difficult study 122; essentially
linked with the notion of *affectus*
116; it is spiritual 116; presupposes
purification 133; spiritual understanding of Scripture is an experience 130; the various steps of
the return to God are experiences
67; method of analyzing spiritual
experience 126–129. The vocabulary of experience: *sentire* 122;
relish 122; a contact 123; contentment and at the same time
yearning 124–125. Mystical experience 131. Spiritual experience
remains myserious 122. Definition:
an inner testimony of the Holy
Spirit 132. Clearly marked aspect
of monastic spirituality 133. One
trait of Aelred's humanism 169.

Form: (*forma*) This word can mean
(1) appearance, beauty, and is

then synonymous with
species 7, 53;
(2) perfection of the image which
has become a likeness; this
form comes from on high
and is wisdom 53. The
whole history of salvation
can be summarized thus:
created man is formed by
God, deformed by sin, re-
formed by the Spirit 53–54;
(3) model: according to St
Ambrose Christ is the form
of friendship (*Am*. 688c,
691b).

Free Will: faculty of *consensus* 11, 16;
is a deliberate choice 11; was
involved in the withdrawal from
God 11–12; is operative in both
good and bad actions 16; man
cannot return to God without
grace, free will alone is not
enough 18.

Friendship: Aelred's teaching on
friendship forms part of his
theology 36–39; this friendship is
spiritual 39; supernatural 38; essentially Christocentric 38–40; raises
man to God 39; forms part of the
plan of salvation 40; the opposition
between cupidity and friendship
40–52.

Fruition: love's final act 31; fruition
defines love which is enjoyment
31; a study of the two aspects of
fruition helps us to understand
better the withdrawal from God
41.

God: God's sabbath is charity 35;
he created by love 35; his proper
work: mercy 43; he has willed
friendship to exist among his
creatures 38; the divine image
gives man a capacity for God 7;
conformity to God is the criterion

of a being's worth 53; God is man's beatitude 32; theocentric anthropology 4.

Image: created in the image of God 4; one of the basic themes of religious thought 4–5; central point of Aelred's doctrine 7, 25; natural image 5; capacity for God 7; the distinction between image and likeness 9; dynamic nature of the image 16; the image remains in a sinner but the likeness is lost 14. Christ restores the image 20; image and friendship 37–38; unity and consistency of Aelred's doctrine 54.

Knowledge: sometimes the antithesis of *sensus* 116; associated with *affectus* in experience-knowledge 116; must be preceded by faith in spiritual understanding 119.

Land of Unlikeness: in Aelred's teaching 12; the idea derives from St Augustine more than from St Bernard 12; experience of wretchedness 126. See *wretchedness.*

Likeness: variable meaning 9; distinction between image and likeness 7–9.

Liturgy: closely associated with Scripture 102; it recalls God's interventions by symbolic actions; what cannot be expressed by words is signified by things (*rebus*) 103. Each phase of the liturgical cycle has its sacrament 104; every liturgical feast involves the past, the present and the future 103; the aim is to arouse devotion 104; liturgy and spiritual experience 131; liturgy and eschatology 157.

Love: importance of this theme in the twelfth century 27; in Aelred

27–28. Love can be described with the aid of images and symbols rather than defined 26; is an *affectus* 29; is perfect when reason accompanies it 117; a natural power 28; analysis of its three elements—election, application to act and fruition 30; special importance of fruition 31; is to be seen in the context of the history of salvation 10, 28.

Mary: inseparable from Christ and his saving work is the Mother of the Savior 23; she is our mother 23; the new Eve, blessed by God and cause of blessings for us 23; the significance of the feast of the Annunciation 23; fullness of grace 23.

Memory: one of the parts of the soul 6; capacity for God 8. Before the fall it had been completely filled by God 10; memory and beatitude 15; its restoration 20.

Mutability: one of the essential characteristics of a creature 11; in the return to God 16.

Nature: theological meaning of the word *nature* in Aelred's doctrine 5–6; can mean only being (*essentia*) 7.

Order (*ordo*), rectification (*ordinatio*): universal law of creation 33–34; importance of this concept in the Middle Ages 16–17; the sinner remains subject to this law 17; virtue is conceived as a rectification 47; cupidity cannot be rectified, it must be destroyed 43; the problem of returning to God is a rectification of charity 10, 44, 82.

Rest: an exigency of the law of order 33–34; charity alone leads to

CISTERCIAN FATHERS SERIES

Under the direction of the same Board of Editors as the CISTERCIAN STUDIES SERIES, the CISTERCIAN FATHERS SERIES seeks to make available the works of the Cistercian Fathers in good English translations based on the recently established critical editions. The texts are accompanied by introductions, notes and indexes prepared by qualified scholars.

Cistercian Publications Spencer Massachusetts 01562
Irish University Press Shannon Ireland